Police and
the Elderly
(PGPS-78)

Pergamon Titles of Related Interest

Bomse   *Practical Spanish for School Personnel, Firemen, Policemen and Community Agencies*

Bouza   *Police Administration: Organization and Performance*

Goldstein et al   *Police Crisis Intervention*

Miron/Goldstein   *Hostage*

Monahan   *Community Mental Health and the Criminal Justice System*

Nietzel   *Crime and Its Modification: A Social Learning Perspective*

O'Brien   *Crime and Justice in America*

Police and the Elderly

Edited by
Arnold P. Goldstein
William J. Hoyer
Phillip J. Monti

Pergamon Press

NEW YORK • OXFORD • TORONTO • SYDNEY • FRANKFURT • PARIS

Pergamon Press Offices:

U.S.A. Pergamon Press Inc., Maxwell House, Fairview Park, Elmsford, New York 10523, U.S.A.

U.K. Pergamon Press Ltd., Headington Hill Hall, Oxford OX3 0BW, England

CANADA Pergamon of Canada Ltd., 150 Consumers Road, Willowdale, Ontario M2J 1P9, Canada

AUSTRALIA Pergamon Press (Aust) Pty. Ltd., P O Box 544, Potts Point, NSW 2011, Australia

FRANCE Pergamon Press SARL, 24 rue des Ecoles, 75240 Paris, Cedex 05, France

FEDERAL REPUBLIC OF GERMANY Pergamon Press GmbH, 6242 Kronberg/Taunus, Pferdstrasse 1, Federal Republic of Germany

Library of Congress Cataloging in Publication Data

Main entry under title:

Police and the elderly.

(Pergamon general psychology series)
1. Police services for the aged—Addresses, essays, lectures. 2. Aged—Crime against—Addresses, essays, lectures. I. Goldstein, Arnold P. II. Hoyer, William J. III. Monti, Philip J.
HV8079.225.P64 1979 364 78-27400
ISBN 0-08-023894-7
ISBN 0-08-023893-9 pbk.

Printed in the United States of America

To Cindy and Susan, with love, respect, and at least a little awe for the people they've become.

A.P.G.

To my parents, Ann and William, who by example have taught the worth of the individual and the joys of growing older.

W.J.H.

To my wife, Carm, whose wonderful commitment of love and wisdom truly inspired this book.

P.J.M.

Contributors

MARGARET M. BRAUNGART
Psychology Department
Syracuse University
Syracuse, New York

RICHARD G. BRAUNGART, Ph.D.
Sociology Department
Syracuse University
Syracuse, New York

ARNOLD P. GOLDSTEIN, Ph.D.
Psychology Department
Syracuse University
Syracuse, New York

PHILIP J. GROSS
Hallcrest Systems, Inc.
7346 Eldorado Street
McLean, Virginia

ROBERT HAMEL
Victims-Witness Assistants Program
District Attorneys Office
Onondaga County Courthouse
Syracuse, New York

WILLIAM J. HOYER, Ph.D.
Psychology Department
Syracuse University
Syracuse, New York

VALAIDA LITTLEJOHN WISE
Psychology Department
Syracuse University
Syracuse, New York

SGT. PHILIP MONTI
Syracuse Police Department
Public Safety Building
Syracuse, New York

ARTHUR PATTERSON, Ph.D.
College of Human Development
Pennsylvania State University
University Park, Pennsylvania

ELIZABETH L. WOLF
2436 University Avenue
Kalamazoo, Michigan

Contents

Preface

The number of elderly citizens in America has risen sharply in recent years, and will continue to rise. With this increase has come a proportionate increase in crime against the elderly, as well as an even greater, disproportionate increase in fear of crime among older citizens. The effective police officer is being called upon more and more to deal in a skilled and sensitive manner with both the fearfulness and the crimes themselves. This book seeks to help the officer in these important tasks.

Crime reduction and reduction of fear of crime can be sought in a variety of ways. We attempt in this book to provide the officer and, through him, the elderly citizen with the knowledge necessary to move toward these goals. Chapter 1 describes what it means to be old in America—both physically and emotionally. This chapter and Chapter 2, which deals with fear of crime among the elderly, provide the officer with information necessary to help him respond to such citizens in a sensitive, patient, and effective manner. These goals of increased effectiveness and increased sensitivity, are more likely to be met if responding officers are aware of the special needs and often severe problems of particular sub-groups of elderly citizens. One such group is the minority elderly, the focus of Chapter 3.

Because it is felt that the best police work is preventive, Chapter 4 presents information that can be used by the officer, or transmitted by him to elderly citizens, to achieve preventive goals.

When preventive techniques fail and a mugging, burglary, or fraud occurs, the officer needs special calming and interviewing techniques in order to conduct a skilled and effective investigation; such techniques are described in detail in Chapter 5.

Once a crime has been committed, responding officers face the dual concern of apprehending the criminal and assisting the victim. Too often an emphasis has been placed on criminal apprehension at the expense of assistance to the victim. Chapter 6 explores a number of ways in which law enforcement personnel can assist elderly crime victims and witnesses.

The two final chapters are concerned with training; Chapter 7 is devoted to training the citizen, and Chapter 8 is concerned with training the police officer. Both describe specific training techniques, materials, and targets to further arm the citizen and the officer with the skills necessary to reduce crime against the elderly, to reduce fear of such crime, and to respond most effectively when such crimes occur.

A.P.G.
W.J.H.
P.J.M.

1 The Elderly: Who Are They?

William J. Hoyer

Gerontology is an interdisciplinary field concerned with the study of aging and the aged. This is an area that has evidenced unprecedented growth in the past few years. The purpose of this chapter is to provide an overview of the growing body of gerontological knowledge for use by police and other law enforcement or criminal justice personnel concerned with crime against the elderly. Special emphasis is placed on the behavioral capabilities and deficiencies of older citizens, and how these might relate to fear of crime, crime prevention, and victimization.

DEMOGRAPHIC CHARACTERISTICS*

Americans like to think of themselves as youthful. Historically, the average age of the American population has been "young." In 1790, when the first census was taken in the United States, half the people were 16 years of age or younger.

*Data reported are based on statistics from the U.S. Department of Health, Education and Welfare and the Bureau of the Census, and on reports by Herman B. Brotman, consultant to the Senate Special Committee on Aging and former assistant to the Commissioner on Aging for HEW.

By 1970, the median age had increased to 28. Over 200 years ago, when the United States declared its independence, life expectancy was approximately 38 years: there were only about 50,000 Americans over age 65, and they constituted a mere 2% of the total population of 2.5 million. By 1900, life expectancy was 48 years, and 3 million older Americans made up approximately 4% of the total population of 80 million.

As of mid-1975, there were approximately 22.4 million persons age 65 or over (Table 1.1), and life expectancy had increased to over 70 years. Older citizens now account for over 10% of the total population. While the proportion of older people in the overall population has more than doubled since 1900, their actual numbers have increased more than sixfold. Table 1.1 projects to the year 2000, when it is expected that there will be 30.6 million older Americans. People over 65 years of age are labeled "elderly" or "aged" for statistical purposes; there is no psychological, biological, or social dividing line at that exact point in the life span. Until quite recently, mandatory retirement began at age 65 for many, and thus "65" has become a chronological sign post for entering old age.

Based on 1974 death rates, overall life expectancy is now greater than 72 years on the average; it is 68.2 for men and close to 8 years longer, 75.9, for women. Between 1960 and 1975, the 65 to 74 age group increased by 26%, while the population of 75 year-olds and older increased by 52%. There are now approximately 2 million Americans who are 85 years of age or older, and about 7500 Americans age 100 or older.

It is estimated that 3600 persons who are 65 or over die every day, and every day 5000 Americans reach age 65. The 1400 per day increase amounts to a yearly increase of 511,000 older persons. However, it is important to

Table 1.1 The Older Population in the Twentieth Century
(age 65 and over)

Year	Total	Men	Women	Ratio Women/Men
1900	3,080,000	1,555,000	1,525,000	98/100
1930	6,634,000	3,325,000	3,309,000	99/100
1970	20,066,000	8,416,000	11,503,000	138/100
1975	22,400,000	9,173,000	13,228,000	144/100
1980	24,523,000	9,914,000	14,609,000	147/100
1985	26,659,000	10,684,000	15,975,000	150/100
1990	28,933,000	11,518,000	17,415,000	151/100
1995	30,307,000	11,995,000	18,311,000	153/100
2000	30,600,000	12,041,000	18,588,000	154/100

differentiate between these "newcomers" and those who are already in the ranks of the elderly. The 7500 living centenarians, for example, were born just after the American Civil War and grew up and grew older in a much different environment than those who are younger. Someone born in 1875 was 20 years old during the Spanish-American War, was 49 years old when Charles A. Lindbergh took off from Roosevelt Field and landed in Paris 33½ hours later, and was over 70 when Babe Ruth announced his retirement on April 27, 1948. Someone who has just become 65 years old was born just before the start of World War I, was 20 during the Great Depression, and was 32 years old when the first atomic bombs exploded over Hiroshima and Nagasaki. As those who are now in their 20s and 30s get older, they, too, will be different in terms of background and behavior than those who are now 65.

Demographers who study population characteristics are very much aware of the impact of age on social, economic and political developments. Government officials are already responding to political pressures from the elderly for new programs and better services (Binstock, 1976). The elderly constitute over 15% of the voting population of the United States, and they are becoming more politically active than ever before. Another economic-political repercussion of the growing elderly population is that pension and Social Security costs to employees and employers will continue to increase; recent federal legislation has increased the Social Security payments of employees and employers to meet some of this demand. In 1945 the ratio of wage earners to Social Security recipients was 35 to 1; today 35 million persons are receiving Social Security, and the ratio of workers to recipients is 3.2 to 1. It is projected that this ratio will fall to an uncomfortable 1.9 to 1 by 2035. The same burden is felt by corporate and other nonfederal pension plans; for example, General Motors Corporation employed 10 workers for every retiree in 1967; this ratio was 4 to 1 in 1978 and it is estimated that it will be 1 to 1 by 2000.

The predominant age group in a society makes a substantial impact on the attitudes and values of that culture. Crime statistics increased dramatically in the 1960s, the years when the children of the post-war "baby boom" were reaching adulthood. The murder rate increased from 4.5 per 100,000 to 6.8 by 1968. Robbery, often the most feared crime because it is usually committed without warning and accompanied by threat or force also increased substantially in the 1960s. In 1959 the robbery rate was 51.2 per 100,000; by 1968 it had more than doubled to 131. Professor Norman B. Ryder, a Princeton University demographer, observed that there is a continuous influx of youth who must be taught to become effective contributors to society. Although past societies and generations have coped with this acculturational task more or less successfully, the sheer numbers of youth reaching adulthood during the decade of the 1960s overwhelmed the various socialization agents—parents, teachers, law enforcers— and social institutions—schools, community organizations—of American society.

Recently, newspaper, magazine, and broadcasting journalists, as well as many policy experts, have painted a very pessimistic social and economic picture by projecting the "baby boom" into the future. At the same time human service occupations have to prepare for increasing numbers of the elderly who must be served in the future. Law enforcement agencies, especially, will have to take changing age trends into account. Many police departments are already experiencing one serious effect of the "graying of America," the increased incidence of crimes against the elderly. Law enforcement officials at all levels must develop community education programs for crime prevention.

Since many crimes are committed by youthful offenders, does the aging trend in American society mean that there will be a decrease in the incidence of crime? Possibly there will be a reduction in the incidence of violent crimes committed against older people; there is some indication of this trend in the most recent *Uniform Crime Reports*. It is also likely that there will be an increase in premeditated crimes such as fraud, which victimize elderly persons. There are some crimes to which the elderly are particularly vulnerable; these will be examined later in this chapter. The elderly themselves commit few crimes—less than 2% of the crimes in the United States are committed by persons over 65—but this might change in the future because of different attitudes and values of succeeding generations of elderly.

HEALTH, INCOME LEVEL, HOUSING, AND OTHER CHARACTERISTICS OF OLDER AMERICANS

According to statistics issued by the Department of Health, Education, and Welfare, only 14% of those 65 or older have no chronic health problems or impairments; however, 82% suffer no limitation of their mobility, regardless of their health condition. Of those 65 or older, 8% have some trouble getting around alone, 6% need a mechanical aid for mobility, and 5% are homebound. People over 65 visit their physicians about twice as often as the rest of the population—8.7 vs. 4.8 visits—and are hospitalized about twice as often. Moreover, their hospital stays on the average last two times as long as those of younger adults—17.5 vs. 8.7 days. Older people have a 25% chance of being hospitalized annually. Annual medical costs for each person over 65 averaged $1,360 in 1975. In comparison, the 1975 per capita cost for persons under 65 totaled $330. Slightly over 60%—$820 of the $1,360—of health care costs of the elderly were assumed by public resources of all kinds, including Medicare and Medicaid. In 1974 Medicare alone covered 38.1%, or about $465 per person, of the total medical costs of older people.

Curiously, the elderly visit the dentist only about half as often as younger adults. Half of the elderly have not been to the dentist in the past five years. Older persons are twice as likely to wear corrective eye glasses and about thirteen times more likely to wear a hearing aid than persons under 65.

The death rate for those over 65 is 61 per 1000—73 for men and 52 for women—compared to 4 per 1000 for those under 65. It is interesting to note, however, that the major part of the increase in average life expectancy in recent years is the result of reduced death rates at birth, in infancy, and during childhood. Because more people now reach old age, the *average* life expectancy has increased. However, those who now reach age 65 do not live much longer than those who reached age 65 in 1900. Three-quarters of all deaths among the elderly are attributable to three diseases: heart disease which claims 46%; cancer, 15%; and stroke, 14%. As most police officers know, elderly men have an unusually high suicide rate; the incidence of male suicides is 0.5 per 100,000 between ages 5 and 14, and rises steadily until it reaches 47.3 per 100,000 at age 85. In contrast, suicide rates for women are highest in middle age, 12.3 per 100,000 between ages 45 and 54, and decline to 4.4 per 100,000 at age 85.

How one plans and accepts aging is an individual matter, but the quality of alternatives available to older people depends upon social and economic policy (Binstock & Shanas, 1976). Some elderly are economically solvent; in 1971 there were 850,000 older couples who had incomes of $15,000 or more, and 1.6 million whose incomes ranged between $10,000 and $15,000. However, 20% of all elderly couples, or 1.1 million, had yearly incomes under $3,000, amounting to less than $58 per week. Some 1.5 million elderly living alone or with non-relatives had incomes under $1500, or $29 per week. Altogether, about 4.3 million older persons, 22% of the 1971 elderly population, lived in households with incomes below the poverty level. Of the 26 million poor in the United States, 16% are 65 years of age or older.

While between 20 and 25% of the aged spend some time as residents of a nursing home or other long term care facility, most people are surprised to learn that only about 1.1 million, or between 4 and 5%, of them actually live in nursing homes, psychiatric facilities, or other institutions. However, the proportion of elderly in institutions increases directly with advancing age; between 20 and 25% of those in the 85+ age group reside in institutions. Between 15 and 20% of Detroit's elderly die in institutions other than general hospitals (Kastenbaum & Candy, 1973). The aged comprise 30% of the population of mental hospitals, but only 2% of the cases seen at outpatient clinics and 4% of those seen at community mental health centers (Kramer, Taube & Redick, 1973). Twice as many women as men are in institutions, but 16% of the older male institutionalized population was in mental hospitals compared with 9% of the elderly female institutionalized population.

Most older people live in a family setting—84% of the men and 59% of the women. Over 33% of the elderly live alone—41% of the women and 17% of the men—and the proportion of those living alone increases rapidly with advancing age. It is interesting to note that most older men are married and most older women are widows. There are four times as many widows as widowers, a fact which is attributable to the sex difference in longevity.

BIOLOGICAL AGING

An older person can usually be recognized by his or her physical characteristics; skin, hair, posture, vitality, and speed of movement will show the effects of aging. Some of these changes occur automatically and irreversibly as part of the aging process, whereas others depend more on external factors such as disease, physical injury, nutrition, and exercise. No person is ever free from the influences of aging, but in old age there is an accelerated rate of change. The temporary aches and pains of young adulthood and middle age are often replaced by persistent ailments. The occasional bad back or trick knee of the 35 year old gradually becomes a constant companion. Many of the health problems of late adulthood are resistant to medical treatment because they stem from an accumulation of many minute physiological changes that have occurred over a lifetime. As already discussed, some diseases and causes of death are more frequent than others in old age. Moreover, there are many gradual changes and many illnesses, such as hardening of the arteries (atherosclerosis), that affect nearly all the elderly living in the United States and other modern industrial societies.

Physical Deterioration

Different cells, organs, and systems develop and deteriorate at different rates. Consider the aging of the brain and the central nervous system. Any brain impairment that inferferes with normal mental functioning is referred to as organic brain syndrome (OBS). Depending on whether the brain damage is temporary or permanent, there are two general types of OBS: acute brain syndromes, which are temporary, and chronic brain syndromes, which are permanent and are marked by progressive impairment. The symptoms of OBS are confusion, short attention span, memory loss, and unpredictable emotions. In many cases it is difficult to determine whether these symptoms are the result of the individual's psychological history and present personal circumstances or whether they are due to actual brain damage. Sometimes mental impairments are more conspicuous and striking in older people because special notice is taken of an older person's mental status. For example, even grandchildren are quick to attribute Granny's occasional forgetfulness to "old age" or "senility" when the same degree of forgetfulness would go unnoticed and unlabeled in someone younger. Similarly, when an older person is forgetful, he comes to think of himself as "losing his marbles," even though his memory may be no worse than it was when he was younger. Such "self-fulfilling prophecies" affect us in many ways.

Stress

Although many of the functions and structures in the biological system of an aging adult are stable, the older person's ability to adjust to change, stress, and illness is quite reduced. The older person reacts more slowly and less completely to internal and external changes. Pulse and respiration return more slowly to normal or resting levels following excitement or exercise as one gets older. This is especially important to consider when dealing with the older person who has just been criminally victimized. He or she might be extremely disoriented, distracted, and confused at the time of the incident. It might take longer to calm the older victim or witness than someone younger.

Sensory Changes

Changes in sensory and perceptual apparatus also occur with advancing age, and the effects limit the older person's ability to identify, avoid, or escape the offender. According to the National Center for Health Statistics, hearing losses affect over 50% of the men and 30% of the women over age 65. Age-related losses are greatest for higher tones, so when interviewing an older person it might be useful to speak—without shouting—in a deeper and louder voice.

Many more of the elderly need eye glasses than do younger persons; and nearly half of all blind people in the United States are 65 or over. The degree of psychological isolation and vulnerability associated with vision loss and other sensory losses is difficult to assess, but it is undoubtedly a large problem. Further, it is not clear now much of an effect vision and hearing losses have on higher mental and psychological functioning. Dr. Leon Pastalan (1968) of the University of Michigan designed eye glass lenses that simulated "old eyes"; objects were blurred, illumination caused glare and discomfort, and floors, walls, and exits were difficult to discriminate unless there was a high degree of color contrast. Thus, the older person may have difficulty in making a positive identification of a suspect or in providing useful descriptive information if lighting at the time of a crime was nonoptimal.

PSYCHOLOGICAL AGING

In recent years a large amount of research has been done on the psychological changes that occur with advancing age, with personality, memory, and intelligence receiving the greatest amount of research attention. How do these psychological dimensions change as we grow older?

Gail Sheehey's (1976) book, *Passages*, and many recent articles in magazines and newspapers indicate a strong public interest in the question of whether personality changes occur during middle adulthood and old age. Psychological change and development are usually seen as taking place throughout life, especially in countries where social and technological changes are as rapid and profound as they have been in the United States. However, the main research finding thus far has been that there is a high degree of continuity in personal characteristics from late adulthood into old age (Kimmel, 1974; Maas &

Kuypers, 1972). In other words, the grouchy, complaining old man was grouchy and complaining in middle age as well, assuming there were no radical changes in his health, life style, or geography.

Memory and intelligence have probably been the most studied of all the psychological dimensions of old age. With regard to memory, researchers have consistently found that there is very little, if any, age-related decline in the ability to remember events of ten years ago. However, short-term memory, such as that which enables one to dial a telephone number without first writing it down, is especially susceptible to weakening with aging. This, of course, could affect the older person's reporting of the details of a crime. Remembering a license plate number might be difficult. Also, when one is surprised or upset, memory is especially unclear; "Oh, it all happened so fast, I don't remember," is a frequent statement.

Many of the intellectual abilities that show a decline with advancing age—the ability to think abstractly, deal competently with numbers, and certain types of reasoning abilities—are relatively unrelated to the reporting of a crime. The victim or witness need not solve the crime! It has been reported that verbal and expressive abilities useful to crime reporting show no decline and may even improve throughout life (Horn, 1976), although the speed with which details can be recounted may decrease with age. An officer who is aware of this can slow things down somewhat for the purposes of effective investigation.

Perhaps the most accurate psychological description of the elderly is one that emphasizes the uniqueness of each older person. As people grow older, the differences between them become accentuated. Some elderly are active and outgoing; others are withdrawn and disengaged. Some are slow mentally, confused, and forgetful; others appear more alert than ever. Police officers and law enforcement personnel at all levels are faced with a full range of personality differences when dealing with elderly persons. For example, Mr. X can be described as follows:

> He can't remember where he put his money, where it came from, or its amount; he is afraid to spend his money sometimes, and other times he squanders it; he wanders from place to place and forgets where he lives; he's living in a condemned building and he's using an old, dangerous portable burner for cooking and heat; he refuses medical and social assistance; he uses the alley window for garbage disposal; and he sometimes yells obscenities at passers-by.

Mr. X might seem familiar, but so might Mr. Y:

> He's always willing to help a neighbor; he visits the senior center on a regular basis; he keeps his apartment safe and neat, albeit cluttered; he sometimes gets overly concerned about crime articles in the newspaper; he always unplugs all appliances when not in use, and strongly encourages others to do likewise.

Everyone is different; each elderly person has his or her past experiences, present physical condition, and unique and visible vulnerabilities.

VICTIMIZATION

Much attention has recently been directed to the problem of criminal victimization, and to whether the older person is uniquely vulnerable to crime. The 1971 White House Conference on Aging prompted many government officials and other professionals to consider this question, and several Congressional subcommittees have held hearings on victimization of the elderly.

Persons 65 years and older are victimized by crimes against their person to a much lesser degree than the total American population. In 1973, the victimization rate was slightly less than 32 per 1000 population. Personal larceny accounted for about 75% of the crimes committed against the elderly. Households headed by someone 65 or older are about half as likely to be burglarized as those headed by someone younger.

Cook and Cook (1976) have examined the question of whether the elderly are more vulnerable than other age groups.

Although there may be little data showing that the impact of crime is more devastating for older citizens, it is likely that this is the case. Also, fear of crime is higher among the elderly than among other age groups (Braungart, Braungart & Hoyer, 1978; Goldsmith & Goldsmith, 1976). However, as Braungart and his colleagues have shown, it is not aging *per se* that accounts for greater fear, but the factors associated with growing old in America—poverty, isolation, and physical fragility—that make for higher levels of fear among the aged.

One reason why elderly persons may have a lower actual incidence of crime is because they are often afraid and avoid risky situations. While it is wise for the elderly not to go out alone in cities at night, there is a point where such fear interferes with life's satisfactions and happiness. Even though caution is exercised, there are certain crimes to which the elderly are particularly vulnerable and to which they fall victim more frequently than other age groups.

Frauds

Someone who is gullible and easily befuddled is a choice target for the confidence artist. The confidence man is clever in selecting victims, and many elderly become targets for his schemes. It is estimated that the total annual "take" from fraudulent activities is about $4 billion, though it is difficult to determine precisely this amount since only about 2% of the victims actually file complaints. When, or if, victims realize they have been "stung," they are frequently too embarrassed or depressed to talk about what happened. Also, victims are likely to feel helpless, hopeless, and that "it's too late" once the crime has been realized, which discourages them from reporting fraud to authorities.

Consumer cons such as discount consumer collectives, aluminum siding and insulation deals, phony mail orders, "earn-money-in-your-own-home" projects, and "get rich overnight" schemes bilk adults of all ages. Some, however, seem deliberately designed to trap the elderly. The "bank examiner" scheme is such a one. The older person receives a telephone call from someone who identifies himself as a bank examiner and says the bank suspects one of the tellers of tampering with the savings accounts. To aid in apprehending the swindler, the victim is asked to go to the bank and withdraw his savings. After returning home with the money, the dupe gets another call from the alleged bank examiner informing him that the bank has caught the teller. The "bank examiner" expresses deep appreciation for the cooperation and offers to send an official messenger to pick up the money and return it to the bank. Of course, the bank messenger shows up, provides the victim with an "official" receipt, and disappears. In 1965 this scheme collected $200,000 from 38 elderly women in Los Angeles.

Older people who are looking forward to spending their retirement years in a warm, sunny far-off place such as Florida or Arizona are especially vulnerable to mail order land sale swindles. Underwater property in Florida and desert wastelands in California have been sold through advertisements that make the location seem like paradise at a bargain, but only "if you act now." These deceptions appeal to the trustworthiness, helpfulness, and good-nature of the victim.

Other schemes take advantage of the older person's special health needs (Bernard, 1965; Young, 1967). For example, arthritis sufferers, many of whom are over 65, spend $300 million yearly on quack remedies. It has been estimated that medical quackery and health swindles, including health foods and vitamin rip-offs, cost the American people about $500 million per year. Vitamins and minerals, which allegedly satisfy the nutritional needs of the elderly, and supplements, which are advertised as preventing or curing various old age diseases, constitute the two main health frauds. Pill salesmen, supposedly backed up by documentation, convince the elderly that their health problems are due to dietary deficiencies that can be remedied by daily doses of overpriced "Vitamin X." Seawater has been sold as a healthful beverage at huge profits. Because the elderly suffer more from various infirmities, they are susceptible to buying "cure-alls" over-the-counter, door-to-door, or by mail order. Whether or not these substances have a positive effect is difficult to assess; often the buyer continues their use because he or she thinks they help. In other words, there may be a placebo effect which maintains the buyer's use of the products. The Senate's special report on frauds and misrepresentation affecting the elderly describes numerous other types of swindles.

Victimization of the Elderly: Why and by Whom?

Many of the urban elderly are most afraid of juvenile gangs. Popular media give great attention to the youthful offender or gang that preys on "little old ladies." In high crime areas, 83% of the crimes against the elderly are, in fact, committed by juvenile delinquents. Gozali (1975) interviewed a group of delinquents charged with criminal actions against the elderly. When he asked why they committed crimes against the elderly, most answered that they are "easy takes."

The judicial system in many states gives special treatment to the youthful offender by disallowing the use of previous records. So, it doesn't take much skill to rip off an 83-year-old woman's purse; the pickings may be small but so is the risk!

Goldsmith (1976), Hahn (1976) and others have discussed many reasons why the elderly are so vulnerable. While 82% of elderly men and 56% of elderly women live in a family setting, 1.4 million elderly men and 4.7 million elderly women live alone. One is more vulnerable to crime when living alone and within the older population the *proportion* living alone increases rapidly with advancing age. The elderly often have experienced losses of physical strength, and are, therefore, unable to run away or to fight back. Perceptual losses, arthritis, and heart conditions contribute to one's perceived and real vulnerability, and make it likely that an older person would be hurt should he try to defend himself; and criminals are aware of the elderly's diminished physical and health status. Older people are visible targets because they are likely to live in "old" neighborhoods that have over the years become high crime areas; thus, the aged are in close proximity to those who victimize them. Further, because the movements of the elderly are relatively predictable, they are predictable victims: they shop on a regular schedule; they generally have fewer non-routine activities, such as guests or parties, than others; pension and Social Security checks arrive on a regular schedule, and so forth. Also older people are likely to depend on public transportation, which puts them in public settings with a high incidence of crime.

ELDERLY CRIMINAL

Even though only 5% of those currently in prison are 45 years of age or older, there has been some work done on characteristics of the older criminal. In Italy, for example, Bisio (1973) noted that aging *per se* does not reduce the likelihood of someone committing a crime. In Japan, where the proportion of elderly offenders is very low, Shimizu (1973) concluded that poverty and unfavorable living conditions are the main causes of crime among the elderly. The most frequent reason for the arrest of elderly Japanese was illegal gambling, followed by defamation and negligent burning; very few felonious crimes or violent crimes were undertaken by the aged. In the United States, the elderly tend to commit crimes of a petty, conniving, or passive nature. Rodstein (1975) noted that chronic brain syndrome may in some cases lead to a loss of inhibitions, which results in inappropriate sexual behavior, quarrelsomeness, shoplifting or "forgetting to pay," and aggressiveness. In court the aged defendant usually blames others or society for his actions. In prison the elderly are usually frightened and dependent, and tend to deteriorate rapidly in the restricted environment; rehabilitation through education and training is very unlikely.

ORGANIZATIONS

A variety of national, state, and local organizations are concerned with the quality of life of elderly persons. Two newly-formed federal agencies, the National Institute of Aging and the Administration on Aging, originally part of the Social Security Administration, are primarily responsible for developing, administering, and funding research and service programs in the biomedical, behavioral, and social sciences. A branch of the National Institutes of Health is also concerned with the quality of mental health services for the elderly. The U.S. Congress, which allocates funds to these organizations, is influenced by the lobbying efforts of the National Retired Teachers Association (NRTA) and the American Association of Retired Persons (AARP), with a combined membership of over 6 million. Professionals in the field of gerontology are represented by the Gerontological Society, with a membership of approximately 5,000 researchers and practitioners from all disciplines. Other oganizations in the field of gerontology are the Association of Gerontologists in Higher Education, American Geriatrics Society, Western Gerontological Society, and various state organizations.* Several colleges and universities have made major commitments to the study of aging and are developing programs in gerontology where students are taking courses in various aspects of aging. Some of the institutions of higher education that have been particularly active in this field are the University of Southern California's Andrus Gerontology Center, Duke University, the University of Chicago, Syracuse University, and Pennsylvania State University.

Some other organizations that have the special interests of the elderly as their focus include: the Elderly Urban Coalition, with delegates in the 50 largest cities in the United States, represents 12 million persons—half the older population—who live in these metropolitan areas; the National Center for the Black Aged and the National Caucus on Black Aged represent minority issues; the National Council of Senior Citizens is interested in legal matters; the National Urban League is an advocacy organization based in New York City; and the Gray Panthers is a growing activist group with branches in several cities. There are other organizations which are concerned especially with crime and the elderly: Law Enforcement Assistance Association, The International Association of Chiefs of Police, and the U.S. Conference of Mayors.

Locally, there are usually a variety of community supportive services available to older citizens. In addition to senior centers, there may be Victim-Witness Assistance Programs, or a representative from the local police department may visit senior centers to discuss crime prevention. In the Syracuse area of New York, for example, there are the following additional organizations for elderly:

ACCORD (Action Coalition to Create Opportunities for Retirement with Dignity) is an activist group;

---

*The names and addresses of the major, national organizations concerned with elderly persons and their welfare appear in Appendix 1, at the end of this chapter.

CALL-A-BUS provides door-to-door bus service for those who find it difficult or impossible to use public transportation;

FISH (Friends in Service Here) provides emergency transportation for shut-ins and emergency housework for the sick;

FOSTER GRANDPARENT PROGRAM unites children who have special needs with the elderly in a warm, one-to-one, helping relationship;

HOME HANDYMAN provides free or low cost home repair services to the isolated elderly, with retirees doing the work;

MEALS ON WHEELS delivers meals to the elderly, ill, or disabled who are unable to prepare nutritious meals; and

TELEPHONE LIFE LINE makes a daily telephone call to those elderly who live alone.

We have tried in this chapter to present information which will provide the reader with a sense of what it is like to be an elderly individual. It is our hope that these many physical, psychological and social details of the aging process will give the reader a useful beginning in better understanding both the remainder of this book and the elderly persons who are our concern here.

APPENDIX 1.
ORGANIZATIONS PERTAINING TO THE ELDERLY

ACTION
806 Connecticut Ave., N.W.
Washington, D.C. 20525
Foster Grandparent Program
Retired Senior Volunteer Program (RSVP)
Service Corp of Retired Executives (SCORE)

Administration on Aging
330 C Street, S.W.
HEW South
Washington, D.C. 20201

Adult Education Association
1225 19th Street
Washington, D.C. 20036

American Association of Retired Persons
1909 K. Street, N.W.
Washington, D.C. 20006

American Geriatrics Society
10 Columbus Circle
New York, New York 10019

Division of Adult Development and Aging (Div. 20)
American Psychological Association
1200 17th Street, N.W.
Washington, D.C. 20036

Gerontological Society
1 Dupont Circle
Washington, D.C. 20036

Gray Panthers
3700 Chestnut Street
Philadelphia, Pennsylvania 19104

National Caucus on the Black Aged
1730 M Street, N.W.
Suite 811
Washington, D.C. 20036

National Center on Black Aged
1730 M Street, N.W.
Suite 811
Washington, D.C. 20036

National Council on the Aging
1828 L Street, N.W.
Suite 504
Washington, D.C. 20036

National Council of Senior Citizens
1511 K Street, N.W.
Washington, D.C. 20005

National Institute on Aging
National Institutes of Health
Public Health Service
Bethesda, Maryland 20014

National Retired Teachers Association
1909 K Street, N.W.
Washington, D.C. 20006

REFERENCES

American Association of Retired Persons and National Retired Teachers Association. *Your retirement anti-crime guide*. Long Beach, Cal.: 1973.

Bernard, V.W. Why people become the victims of medical quackery. *American Journal of Public Health*, 1965, *55*, 1142-1147.

Binstock, R.H. & Shanas, E. (Eds.) *Handbook of aging and the social sciences*. New York: Van Nostrand Reinhold, 1976.

Bisio, B. Data on antisocial behavior in the elderly. *Ospedale Psichiatrico (Napoli)*, 1973, *41*, 219-242.

Braungart, M.M., Braungart, R.G. & Hoyer, W.J. Age, sex, and social factors in fear of crime. Paper presented at the meeting of the Southern Sociological Society, 1978.

Cook, F.L. & Cook, T.D. Evaluating the rhetoric of crisis: A case study of criminal victimization of the elderly. *Social Service Review*, 1976, *50*, 632-646.

Goldsmith, J. Community crime prevention and the elderly: A segmented approach. *Crime Prevention Review*, 1975, *2*, 18-19.

Goldsmith, J. & Goldsmith, S. *Crime and the elderly*. Lexington, Mass.: D.C. Heath, 1976.

Gozali, J. Improving safety of elderly persons in high crime areas. *The Gerontologist*, 1975, *15*, 82.

Hahn, P.H. *Crimes against the elderly: A study of victimology*. Santa Cruz, Cal.: Davis Publishing Co., 1976.

Horn, J.L. Organization of data on life-span development of human abilities. In L.R. Goulet & P.B. Baltes (Eds.) *Life-span developmental psychology*. New York: Academic Press, 1970.

Hudson, R.B. & Binstock, R.H. Political systems and aging. In R.H. Binstock and E. Shanas (Eds.) *Handbook of aging and the social sciences*. New York: Von Nostrand Reinhold, 1976.

Kastenbaum, R. & Candy, S.E. The 4% fallacy: A methodological and empirical critique of extended care facility population statistics. *International Journal of Aging and Human Development*, 1973, *4*, 15-21.

Kimmel, D.C. *Adulthood and aging*. New York: Wiley, 1974.

Kramer, M., Taube, C. & Redick, R. Patterns of use of psychiatric facilities by the aged: Past, present, future. In C. Eisdorfer & M.P. Lawton (Eds.), *The psychology of adult development and aging*. Washington, D.C.: American Psychological Association, 1973.

Mass, H.S. & Kuypers, J.A. *From thirty to seventy*. San Francisco: Jossey-Bass, 1974.

Pastalan, L.A., Mautz, R.K. & Merrill, J. The simulation of age-related losses: A new approach to the study of environmental barriers. In W.F.E. Preiser (Ed.) *Environmental design research, Vol. 1*. Stroudsberg, Pa.: Powden, Hutchinson & Ross, 1973.

Rodstein, M. Crime and the aged: 2. The criminals. *Journal of the American Medical Association*, 1975, *234*, 639.

Sheehey, G. *Passages: Predictable crises of adult life*. New York: Dutton, 1976.

Shimizu, M. A study on the crimes of the aged in Japan. *Aeta Criminologae Et Medicinae Legalis Japonica*, 1973, *39*, 202-213.

Young, J.H. *The medical messiahs*. Princeton, N.J.: Princeton University Press, 1967.

2 Fear of Crime and the Elderly

Margaret M. Braungart
William J. Hoyer
Richard G. Braungart

Concern over rising crime rates has created a life of fear for many elderly people in this country. Newspaper accounts and stories tell of robberies, beatings, and assaults involving elderly victims, some of whom are over 80 years old. Many of the elderly living in large cities do not go out after dark; it's safer not to visit children or friends, not to go to the drugstore or grocery, not to attend a movie or meeting. Afraid someone will rob or hurt them, older citizens increasingly remain behind bolted doors and forego many of the experiences that give joy and meaning to life. On the day Social Security checks are to be delivered, elderly people can be seen huddled in city doorways waiting for their checks and worrying about the muggers and swindlers who are also waiting (Bonner, 1977). A few of the elderly are so frightened they take tranquilizers regularly; others are forced to pay extortion money for protection. The most dramatic story came from the Bronx in New York, where Hans and Emma Kabel—an elderly immigrant couple who had been robbed twice and attacked once—hung themselves because they could not bear another day of fear (Bonner, 1977; Graham, 1977).

Are the elderly in this country overly frightened about crime? Are older people much more likely to be afraid of crime than the young and middle-aged? The purpose of this chapter is to provide a clear perspective on the problem of fear of crime among the elderly in the United States. First, the extent of fear of crime is discussed for the population as a whole and for the elderly in particular. Second, some of the explanations often given for fear among older citizens are reviewed, along with some of the research describing the characteristics of those older persons who are especially likely to be afraid of crime. Finally, information is presented concerning the effects of fear on older persons and the various attempts that have been made to reduce fear of crime among the elderly.

FEAR OF CRIME IN THE UNITED STATES

National polls have indicated that fear of crime currently ranks as a major concern in the United States, particularly among the elderly. In a recent Gallup survey, those living in cities with populations over 500,000 listed crime as the number one social problem. By comparison, only 4% of the people surveyed in a 1949 Gallup poll ranked crime as a major social problem (Pope & Feyerherm, 1976). In reviewing a number of surveys and national opinion polls conducted over the past 10 years, Erskine (1974) concluded that the fear of being victimized has increasingly become a major problem to the city resident, the poor, and the aged. A 1974 Harris poll, commissioned by the National Council on Aging, surveyed the problems of the elderly and reported that fear of crime was the most serious concern for persons over 65, followed by poor health and inadequate finances (Harris, 1974).

In a 1976 nationwide survey, 50% of older people claimed they were afraid to walk in their own neighborhoods, while approximately 40% of young and middle-aged citizens indicated fear. In comparison with an earlier 1974 survey, the percentage of fearful elderly showed a greater increase than that of young and middle-aged adults (Braungart, Braungart, & Hoyer, 1978; Lebowitz, 1975). The question can be raised whether there is something special about being older that makes elderly people more fearful and apprehensive over crime.

Reasons for Fear of Crime Among the Elderly
A number of explanations have been offered as to why older people are more frightened at the thought of becoming crime victims than younger age groups. These explanations concern physical factors, social factors, psychological interpretations, and situational or environmental conditions.

Physical Factors. Certain physical changes occur as people age that may make them feel weaker or more vulnerable and, therefore, easier targets for the criminal. Although only 14% of the elderly people in the United States are classified as disabled, about 85% suffer from one or more chronic illnesses which usually limit their normal, everyday activities in some way (Lawton, Nahemow, Yaffee, & Feldman, 1976; Shanas, 1971). Activity is more restricted for women than men, and for those from lower socioeconomic backgrounds (Shanas & Maddox, 1976). Yet, only 5% of the elderly population are institutionalized; the overwhelming majority manage to function within their communities (U.S. Bureau of the Census, 1976). In fact, a survey of elderly residents in one community found that 90% considered themselves self-sufficient (Wolf, 1977). This suggests that, while the elderly may well have illnesses, aches, and pains, they live with these infirmities as best they can in an independent manner.

Aging is often accompanied by visual and hearing losses and by a decline in muscle strength and coordination, all of which affect a person's ability to process information and react quickly (Kimmel, 1974). While intelligence testing of elderly people indicates that verbal ability and long-term memory remain remarkably stable, it also suggests that there is often a slowing down in speed of performance and a difficulty in using old information to solve new problems (Botwinick, 1973; Kimmel, 1974). These declines in reaction time and the ability to process information help us to understand why the elderly are likely to feel vulnerable and fearful in threatening situations where things happen very quickly. They may be especially frightened about being attacked, mugged, or robbed; and they may appear confused when reporting a criminal incident to the police.

Social Factors. Another reason older people are particularly fearful about crime may be partially caused by the fact that not much value is placed on growing old in American society, and so the aged may lose some of their feelings of esteem and self-worth (Riley & Waring, 1976). Unfortunately, negative stereotypes and images of growing old exist. Aging may be associated with declines in physical attractiveness, sexual prowess, health, and vigor, as well as with impending death. Of course, some persons who are most hostile to the aged are those who are especially fearful of their own eventual decline and demise (Streib, 1976). Because our culture places primary emphasis on occupation as a means of classifying and ranking individuals, retirees may be viewed, or may even view themselves, as nonproductive and a burden. In America, social and technological change is emphasized and the wisdom of the past is frequently given little weight; in effect, the elderly are "put out to pasture." Consequently, older people may feel alone, isolated, and segregated from the mainstream (Riley & Waring, 1976). In such an atmosphere, it is not surprising that gangs of adolescents and swindlers systematically rip-off elderly people, or that the elderly victims consider themselves as "unworthy" of police concern.

Another social factor affecting the elderly's fear of crime is America's highly mobile society. Because of retirement moves and changing neighborhoods, older people may no longer live near their children, families, and old friends. Elderly persons, especially those living in large cities, often find themselves in a neighborhood of strangers where there is likely to be considerable moving in and out. This lack of neighborhood stability can create feelings of isolation and fear.

Social contacts and the intimate emotional experiences of life may become restricted as aging progresses. As one experiences the loss of a spouse, relatives, and friends through disease and death, feelings of loneliness and fear can intensify. Elderly women are often more isolated than older men: 80% of the men over 65 are married, and only 15% of those remaining live alone; in contrast, only 35% of the women over 65 are married, and 33% of those remaining live alone (U.S. Bureau of the Census, 1976).

Economic loss and financial deprivation are other social problems that can heighten an older person's feelings of vulnerability and fear. Life can be especially difficult for the older person who finds financial resources inadequate to meet daily needs. While the median income for all families in the United States in 1974 was $12,836, the median income for families with the head of household over 65 was $7,298 (U.S. Bureau of the Census, 1976). Approximately 16% of the total elderly population and 36% of the elderly blacks are below the poverty level. Although the incomes of those over 65 are about half those of the younger population, the elderly spend about four times more on medical care than younger age groups (Sicker, 1977). At each age level, women are more likely to be poor (Schultz, 1976) and to have to face the problems of poor housing, inadequate transportation, and poor nutrition.

The effects of being poor may be more frightening to older persons living in decaying urban areas, which greatly increase feelings of vulnerability, isolation, and fear. In fact, over 50% of the elderly in the United States live in urban areas, and 62% of these live in decaying central cities. The figures are even more pronounced for elderly blacks; 66% live in urban areas, and 85% of them are concentrated in central cities (U.S. Bureau of the Census, 1976). Many central cities are characterized by deteriorating social and economic conditions, and by high crime rates (Cohen & Short, 1976). The elderly who live in crime-infested areas may feel they cannot afford to move, may be in need of public housing, or may even be afraid to move (Patterson, 1977). The urban elderly poor often find themselves isolated. Drugstores and grocery stores refuse to deliver; cabs will not come; doctors neither set up practices nor make house calls; and grown children may not want to risk the visit home (Conklin, 1976; Lawton, Nahemow, Yaffee, & Feldman, 1976).

Psychological Factors. Old age, the final stage of life, can be either a time of self-acceptance or a time of despair and dissatisfaction, as the aging person reflects over his or her past accomplishments and faces death (Erikson, 1968). Those who despair of their own lives are often unhappy and fearful. As some people grow older they tend to withdraw from activities and relationships, thus lowering their morale and increasing their feelings of personal isolation (Maddox, 1965). Whether or not an older person feels a part of life and society is strongly influenced by good health, an out-going personality, social activities, and the presence of someone in whom he or she can confide (Botwinick, 1973). Although the personality does not usually undergo major changes in later life, some older people may experience a turning inward; they may become more rigid, and feel a decline in both energy and emotion (Botwinick, 1973).

In general, elderly people are not faced with major emotional disturbances just because they grow older. However, it should be recognized that old age is a time of great adjustment—as is adolescence. The elderly must accommodate to a number of changing circumstances in life—retirement, physical decline, personal loss of loved ones, changing social roles, deteriorating resources, and, possibly, negative attitudes toward their condition. Perhaps the elderly should be given more credit for faring so well in the face of often severe physical, social, and personal losses. Those older persons whose life situations are especially difficult might be expected to feel more vulnerable to victimization than those whose health, financial resources, and social contacts are positive and supportive.

Situational or Environmental Factors. The environment surrounding the older person can influence his or her feelings of fear. The rapidly rising crime rate creates uncertainty among older citizens used to a slower, safer way of life; and the fears of older persons living in decaying, high crime neighborhoods appear to be justified. In fact, a 1972 Gallup poll found that 33% of the people living in densely-populated center cities reported having been mugged, robbed, or the victims of vandalism during that year (Mauss, 1975). Crime tends to flourish in poor neighborhoods were social ties are weak (Cohen & Short, 1976; Conklin, 1976); and certain sections of many large cities are often characterized as having a poor economic base and high mobility. Where neighbors remain strangers, there are few informal social controls—often the most effective way of discouraging criminal activity (Cohen & Short, 1976; Conklin, 1976).

Situational factors may include stories one hears or reads about elderly people being victimized. For example, it must have been frightening to an older person in the Washington, D.C. area to read a *Washington Post* headline, "Youthful Gang Accused of Victimizing 112 Elderly" (Daniels, 1977). The article described how teams of youth gangs systematically stalked elderly people from shopping areas to their homes; there, the victims were robbed, assaulted, and often injured. The situation becomes even more frightening to the older person when he or she begins to hear from a friend or neighbor about the elderly lady down the street who was mugged, or the old man three blocks away whose home was vandalized and heavily damaged.

Not all elderly people feel weak, vulnerable, or frightened over crime, but it is important to identify those groups who are especially fearful so that they may be helped. A number of research investigations have been conducted in this area; they suggest that sex, race, living conditions, and the direct experience of having been a victim of crime are related to whether or not older persons are afraid of crime.

SOCIAL CHARACTERISTICS RELATED TO FEAR OF CRIME

Sex
Most surveys on the fear of crime indicate that women are about twice as likely as men to report being afraid (Braungart, Braungart, & Hoyer, 1978; Clemente &

Kleiman, 1976; Lebowitz, 1975; Sundeen & Mathieu, 1975). While a number of studies have found that approximately 60% of all elderly women are frightened over crime, certain groups appear highly fearful. Over 80% of those elderly women who are black, unmarried, living alone, and dissatisfied with their health, or who had been burglary victims in the past, expressed fear of crime (Braungart, Braungart, & Hoyer, 1978). This study demonstrated that sex differences relating to fear of crime are much greater than age differences.

Race

Race is another factor related to fear of crime; elderly blacks are more likely to be fearful over crime than whites. While 70% of all blacks over the age of 60 expressed fear about walking in their neighborhoods, only 49% of the whites expressed comparable fear of their own neighborhoods (Braungart, Braungart, & Hoyer, 1978). Further examination revealed some interesting differences within racial categories. While few young black males or females expressed fear, approximately 80% of middle-aged and older black women and 59% of elderly black males appeared fearful. White women at each age level were much more likely to report fear than men, and, surprisingly, as many young white women under the age of 30 expressed fear—64%—as did elderly white women over the age of 60—63%. This suggests that it is not only elderly women who are highly anxious about crime, but young white women as well.

Health Status

There also appears to be a relationship between health status and fear of crime. Individuals who considered themselves in good health and physical condition were found to be less fearful than those who were not satisfied with their health. The effects of health appear to be more important for older women than men. While 67% of the females and 40% of the males who were in fair health and 72% of the females and 40% of the males who were in poor health expressed fear, only 59% of the females and 29% of the males who were satisfied with their health had this reaction (Braungart, Braungart, & Hoyer, 1978).

Living Conditions

A number of different studies suggest that the living conditions of elderly people affect their fear of crime. Fearfulness has been found to be associated with rural-urban residence, dwelling arrangements and marital status. Several surveys indicated that urban dwellers are more likely to be anxious about crime than rural residents—the larger the city, the greater the fear of crime (Lebowitz, 1975). In fact, 71% of the national sample of elderly citizens living in large cities were afraid, while only 19% of the rural elderly claimed they were apprehensive over crime. Another survey of two communities in Boston indicated that elderly residents were much more frightened about crime than younger groups, and those elderly who lived in a high crime section of the city were extremely anxious (Conklin, 1976). However, in a more recent study, rural-urban differences appear to be shifting. While fear was expressed by 61% of the elderly living in middle-size cities and suburban areas, only 54% of those living in large cities, 48% in small cities, and 47% in rural areas voiced apprehension. Perhaps the recent spread of crime into the suburbs may account for this increased fearfulness among elderly residents of middle-size cities and suburban areas (Braungart, Braungart, & Hoyer, 1978).

Several research studies examined large cities to determine whether dwelling arrangements make a difference in older people's fear of crime. It was found that people living in retirement communities and condominiums were most likely to feel safe, while those living in areas with a high proportion of minority groups expressed the greatest fear (Sundeen and Mathieu, 1975). Although it is a popular notion that older people should live among different age groups rather than in age-segregated housing, research evidence suggests that elderly people living with other older people feel the safest. A study of Albany, New York residents living in public housing projects reported that the elderly living in age-segregated housing expressed less fear than those living in mixed-age housing projects (Sherman, Newman, & Nelson, 1976).

With regard to living arrangements and fearfulness, several studies indicated that older people who live alone are much more anxious and fearful about crime than those who live with other people (Lebowitz, 1975). Another investigation revealed that elderly women living alone were especially fearful and much more likely to report being afraid than older men living alone. However, both older men and women who had never married were found to be a highly fearful group, with over 80% reporting they were anxious about crime (Braungart, Braungart, & Hoyer, 1978). Over 75% of the middle-aged and elderly women who were separated, divorced, or widowed reported that they were afraid to walk in their neighborhoods. Married older women were less likely to express fear, and married elderly men seldom indicated fear. These findings regarding living arrangements and marital status support the view that living under relatively isolated circumstances increases feelings of fear and anxiety over crime.

Previous Victims of Crime

Much of the literature in the area of fear of crime indicates that elderly people who have previously been the victims of crime are especially fearful. The effects of being burglarized have been found to be much more devastating among women than men. In a nationwide survey, 85% of the elderly women who had previously been victimized reported being afraid (Braungart, Braungart, & Hoyer, 1978).

These research studies on fear of crime point out that, while the elderly in general are somewhat more likely than younger and middle-aged persons to express fear of crime, certain groups of elderly citizens are especially fearful in our society. The most seriously threatened appear to be center-city residents, women, blacks, those in poor health, older people living alone, the unmarried, those living in age-mixed public housing in large cities, and the recent victims of crime. Sex has been found to be a consistently important factor associated with fear of crime; elderly women in each of the above categories are more apprehensive over crime than elderly men. In addition, there is recent evidence that fear of crime is growing among elderly residents of rural and suburban areas, and that young white women who live alone also feel threatened by crime.

EFFECTS OF FEAR OF CRIME

Groups of frightened elderly people in the United States can have serious consequences for both the fearful individual and the community. Fearfulness can severely limit activities and mobility among the aged. One survey found that 54% of the older people interviewed claimed that they changed their pattern of living to avoid becoming victims of crime (Cairns, 1977). When compared with younger age groups, elderly people were much more likely to take precautions against crime, often restricting their social contacts and activities in response to their fears (Conklin, 1976; Lawton, Nahemow, Yaffee, & Feldman, 1976). In another study, nearly 75% of the elderly respondents surveyed said that fear of crime had hampered their freedom of movement and activity (Wolf, 1977). Fear of crime, then, may seriously restrict the quality of life for the elderly and, no doubt, increase their feelings of dissatisfaction and alienation (Goldsmith & Tomas, 1974; Lebowitz, 1975). The older person's fear of becoming a victim of crime can have a "chilling" effect, with some elderly so frightened they become prisoners in their own homes, living a life of "self-imposed house arrest" (Conklin, 1976; Goldsmith & Tomas, 1974).

Perhaps one of the saddest stories came from the Bronx policeman who told reporters about "Mary." Mary was 75 years old and, after being mugged, never left her apartment. She was so frightened that she did not even carry out the garbage, which accumulated day-by-day, month-by-month. Systematically, each room in her apartment was filled with garbage and then sealed. Mary did not go out for food; she tossed money out the window to children who bought her candy bars. Even the children abused her by overcharging for the candy. One day Mary let down her guard and went out to mail a letter. She was mugged again. It was only then that the police learned about her plight and the devastating effect of fear on her life (Graham, 1977).

Fear of crime not only has serious consequences for the frightened citizen, but it actually contributes to the crime problem in the wider community as well. Fear tends to divide people and isolate them from each other. Instead of reaching out to others for support and pressuring the community for protection, many fearful citizens withdraw from social contact and responsibility in their attempt to protect themselves. This kind of response, in fact, helps the criminal in his or her job. It has been well documented that people living in high crime areas are less likely to report crimes to the police than those living in low crime communities (Cohen & Short, 1976; Conklin, 1976). Residents of high crime areas are also more likely to feel that fighting crime is the responsibility of the police and to rely completely on law enforcement agencies to stop crime (Conklin, 1976). A survey by the National Organization of Retired Persons reported that 55% of the elderly respondents did not report crimes because they felt police were ineffective (Greenstein, 1977). However, a recent government-sponsored study of victimization in eight major cities found that older and female victims were much more likely to report crimes to the police than younger and male victims (Hindelang, 1976). In all age groups, the most common reasons given for not reporting a crime were, "Nothing could be done," or "It was not important enough."

It has been suggested that part of the reason why old people may not report crimes is a general lack of information concerning the criminal justice system. Police are strangers; misconceptions are drawn from television dramas about police and law enforcement; people are not certain of the procedures for reporting a crime. Older people may even feel ashamed because they were victims; perhaps they were careless or feel they were justifiably punished for doing a "foolish thing" such as going out after dark, leaving a door unlocked, or carrying too much money with them on an errand (Greenstein, 1977).

Research has been conducted to determine the characteristics of those elderly who reported crimes to police and those who did not. One study in Dallas found that older people who reported crimes felt a sense of control over their lives and a strong sense of social responsibility. They often reported the crime immediately after it occurred or was discovered, and they were not likely to seek the advice of others before reporting. Those elderly who did not report crimes were described as feeling they had little control over their lives and little sense of social responsibility; further, they tended to seek the advice of others before taking action. Nonreporters often felt that the greater the amount of money that was involved in the crime, the more likely that the police would be responsive. Some of the reasons they gave for not reporting were: the crime was not important enough; they could not prove who did it, or they did not have enough useful information; the police would not, or could not, do anything about it; and they feared the criminal would seek revenge (Baggett, 1977).

Fear of crime is pervasive among elderly, especially among older women. Fear of crime takes its toll on the frightened person's quality of life and on the community, demoralizing the individual and hampering law enforcement. Is the level of fearfulness among older people reasonable, or are older citizens misreading the actual probability of being victimized?

PERCEIVED VERSUS ACTUAL VICTIMIZATION
AMONG THE ELDERLY

The evidence suggests that far more elderly persons are frightened about crime than are actually victimized. The elderly have especially strong fears about being murdered or raped. In reality, there is a very low probability that they will be victims of these violent acts (Dussich & Eichman, 1976; Hindelang, 1976). Two factors appear to be involved in the older person's assessment of the situation: first, they calculate the probability of their being victimized in the light of their environments; and second, they assess their personal ability to handle a threatening situation in the light of their personal feelings of vulnerability (Lawton, Nahemow, Yaffee, & Feldman, 1976).

It is difficult to obtain national statistics on victimization. Most of our information has come from surveys conducted in cities scattered throughout the United States. A Department of Justice survey of households in eight large cities found that as age increases, the likelihood of personal or household victimization decreases. Thus, the elderly generally have a lower rate of victimization for most crimes against persons or property. When older people do become victims of crime, the offenses are more likely to be against property than persons. The offender is frequently a male under the age of 24 who is a stranger to the victim. In fact, older people have a much greater likelihood of being victimized by strangers than do young people (Hindelang, 1976). The age group over 65 has the lowest rate of personal victimization of all age groups in society. Within the elderly age bracket, the victimization rate is highest for black females, followed closely by that for white females, and lowest for both white and black males (Hindelang, 1976).

Marital status appears to be an important factor here; among the elderly, the highest rate of personal victimization was suffered by the divorced or separated and, to a somewhat lesser degree, by those who never married. Those who were married had the lowest rate of victimization (Hindelang, 1976). While the overall victimization rates for the elderly remain considerably lower than those for younger age groups, older people are particularly susceptible to purse-snatching, robbery with injury, personal larceny, and swindling (Dussich & Eichman, 1976; Lawton, Nahemow, Yaffee, & Feldman, 1976).

Although one often thinks of "street-crimes" when talking about crimes against the elderly, bunco and confidence games are major threats that are frequently directed specifically at the elderly. In fact, the San Francisco and Los Angeles police departments reported that over 90% of the bunco victims were over 65, and most of these were women (Younger, 1976). Large-scale frauds are directed at the more affluent elderly, while the small bunco scheme is directed at the poor, inner-city aged (Geis, 1976).

The elderly are swindled in many ways: they are presented with economic schemes such as pre-paid funeral planning, health insurance, income security programs, and welfare and Social Security check frauds; they are subjected to medical quackery and "get-well-quick" plans; they are deceived by mail-order frauds such as "work-at-home" deals, franchises, and retirement real estate; and they are cheated in home and automobile repair deals (Geis, 1976; Sicker, 1977). Nursing home scandals and Medicare rip-offs represent a massive defrauding of both the elderly and the general public. While many of these schemes involve loss of money, perhaps the most serious are the medical frauds that are harmful to health and tend to delay visits to physicians.

While statistics suggest that the elderly are not victimized to any greater extent than younger age groups, the effect of victimization seems to have a much stronger and more frightening impact on an older person's life. Because many elderly victims are poor, the consequences of being robbed, burglarized, or swindled can be catastrophic. Young people can recover their losses by earning extra money; old people often cannot. If attacked, older people are likely to suffer more serious and long-lasting injuries. The psychological impact of being victimized appears greater also. Crimes such as purse-snatching and "bunco" schemes rely upon the victim's vulnerability (Goldsmith & Goldsmith, 1976). These crimes are sometimes referred to as "crib-jobs"—"taking candy from a baby."

Elderly victims may become more incensed over the unfairness of the crime and the humiliation they suffered than over the crime itself (Lawton, Nahemow, Yaffee, & Feldman, 1976). It has been said that a little bit of the older person seems to die after having been victimized. As an example, consider one 77-year-old widow in the Bronx. Over a two-year period she was burglarized three times and mugged twice. In one incident a girl held a knife to her throat and demanded a family ring from her finger. When the widow told the girl it was only a trinket from the dime store, the girl flung the old woman against the wall crying, "Choke on it!" At another time someone threw a flare into her apartment window and burned out the entire room. It is small wonder that the widow is lonely, depressed, takes tranquilizers, and seldom ventures outside her apartment (Graham, 1977). Police sensitivity to the fears of an elderly victim can be extremely important in the police-victim relationship.

REDUCING FEAR OF CRIME AMONG THE ELDERLY

The elderly in society represent a special group, primarily because of their vulnerability. Although they are not victimized more than other age groups in society, the effects of victimization are especially devastating to older people. They may be unable to replace the lost money or the damaged property, and they may take a long time to recover from personal injury. There appears to be little doubt that many elderly women are frightened about becoming victims and restrict their lives because of their fears. What can be done to improve the situation?

As the ranks of the elderly have grown and their awareness of their position in society has increased, special groups have been organized to articulate and advocate their needs. The aged represent a special social group who must vie for services and resources to meet their concerns. There is a movement afoot to protect the elderly from crime and to view their victimization as a particularly noxious aspect of the rising crime rate (Sykes, 1976).

To protect themselves against crime and to combat widespread fears, the elderly have organized themselves in a number of ways and have requested and received help from a variety of community service programs. Recognizing, too, that the community and police cannot do all the work needed to stop crime, elderly people have begun to rely on each other to fight crime and fear. In some cities public housing projects are segregated by age. As studies indicate, this helps older residents to feel more secure. Some of them have taken further steps to discourage criminals. Residents often remain in groups in the lobby or outside on the steps, questioning strangers who enter the building; or the system may be more formalized, with volunteer squads patrolling the hallways and the street. In these situations, social contact among older residents is increased, isolation and anonymity are minimized, threat and fear are reduced, and the criminal's job is made more difficult. Since criminals often evaluate whether it is worth the effort to attempt a crime under these conditions, some of these informal measures can be among the most effective in preventing crime (Cohen & Short, 1976).

A variety of volunteer programs have been organized to help reduce fear among the elderly; escort services, sometimes manned by high school students, are available; seniors act as liaison between the police and the community; court cases are monitored to see that justice is carried out in cases involving senior victims (Graham, 1977). Recent evidence suggests these programs may be effective; a 25% reduction in crime involving elderly persons was reported in New York City in 1977. The Police Commissioner of New York City attributed the reduction largely to the elderly themselves, to expanded programs within the police department, and to the courts that dealt more sternly with those guilty of committing crimes against elderly citizens (Buder, 1977).

SUMMARY

There is little doubt that elderly people in the United States are becoming increasingly frightened about becoming targets of crime, and they are more likely to express this fear than are younger age groups. A variety of explanations has been offered to account for this mounting fear: physical declines that accompany the process of aging, cultural attitudes and personal feelings of social vulnerability, environmental or situational factors, and psychological interpretations having to do with changing roles, emotions, and personality needs. Older people may feel vulnerable and isolated, and, therefore, more frightened about being victimized than younger age groups. In a sense, they have more to lose if they are robbed, injured, or swindled.

Research in the area of fear of crime among the elderly identified certain groups who are especially likely to be afraid: older women, blacks, center-city residents, those living in mixed-age public housing projects in high crime areas, the unmarried or those living alone, and previous victims of crime. Fear was greatest among those who were in a disadvantaged social position, had poor health, and maintained few social contacts in their living arrangements. However, regardless of social characteristics, women are far more likely than men to report fear of crime.

When older people are threatened by crime, both they and the society suffer. As frightened individuals restrict their everyday lives in an effort at self-protection, social contacts lessen within the neighborhood and the opportunity for effective informal social control against criminals declines. Policemen's work is more difficult in neighborhoods where there is fear not only because they bear the entire burden for crime prevention, but also because frightened people frequently do not report crimes.

In general older people do not stand a greater probability of being victimized than younger age groups. If victimized, the elderly appear to be the targets of special crimes such as swindling, personal theft without injury, and larceny; there is a much lower probability they will be the victims of violent crimes.

Some efforts have already been made to get at the problem of fear of crime. The elderly themselves have organized in some cases to patrol buildings and streets, act as liaison with the police, and monitor court cases. In addition, police in cities around the country have developed educational programs to provide information on crime prevention and have followed these up with home security checks. Volunteer programs have been established to escort older people on shopping and recreational expeditions; and victim-assistance programs have been set up to help the older person who does become victimized. Recent evidence in New York City suggests that these efforts may be partially effective in reducing crime.

REFERENCES

American Association of Retired Persons & National Retired Teachers Association. *Your retirement anti-crime guide*. AARP & NRTA, Long Beach, California, 1973.

Baggett, S. & Ernst, M. From research to application: Development of police and older adult training modules. *Police Chief*, 1977, *44*, 51-53.

Bild, B.R. & Havighurst, R.J. Senior citizens in great cities: The case of Chicago. *The Gerontologist*, 1976, *16*, 4-88.

Bonner, A. Fear of crime limits activities of the aged. *The Washington Post*, May 4, 1977, B-7.

Botwinick, J. *Aging and Behavior*. New York: Springer, 1973.

Braungart, M.M., Braungart, R.G. & Hoyer, W.J. Age, sex, and social factors in fear of crime. Paper presented at the Meeting of the Southern Sociological Society, New Orleans, 1978.

Brostoff, P.M. The police connection: A new way to get information and referral services to the elderly. In J. Goldsmith & S. Goldsmith (Eds.) *Crime and the elderly*, Lexington, Mass.: Lexington Books, 1976.

Buder, L. Assaults on the elderly off 25% since Jan. 1. *New York Times*, July 3, 1977, 1 & 25.

Clemente, F. & Kleiman, M.B. Fear of crime among the aged. *Gerontologist*, 1975, *17*, 321-327.

Cohen, A. & Short, J.F., Jr. Crime and juvenile delinquency. In R.K. Merton & R. Nisbet (Eds.), *Contemporary social problems*. New York: Harcourt Brace Jovanovich, 1976.

Conklin, J.E. Robbery, the elderly, and fear: An urban problem in search of a solution. In J. Goldsmith & S. Goldsmith (Eds.) *Crime and the elderly*. Lexington, Mass.: Lexington Books, 1976.

Cunningham, C.L. Pattern and effect of crime against the aging: The Kansas City study. In J. Goldsmith & S. Goldsmith (Eds.) *Crime and the elderly*. Lexington, Mass.: Lexington Books, 1976.

Daniels, L.A. Youthful gang accused of victimizing 112 elderly. *The Washington Post*, February 24, 1977, B-1.

Dussich, J.P. & Eichman, C.J. The elderly victim: Vulnerability to the criminal act. In J. Goldsmith & S. Goldsmith (Eds.) *Crime and the elderly*. Lexington, Mass.: Lexington Books, 1976.

Erikson, E. *Identity: Youth and crisis*. New York: Norton, 1968.

Erskine, H. The polls: Fear of violence and crime. *Public Opinion Quarterly*, 1974, *38*, 131-145.

Furstenburg, F. Public reactions to crime in the streets. *American Scholar*, 1971, 601-610.

Geis, G. Defrauding the elderly. In J. Goldsmith & S. Goldsmith (Eds.) *Crime and the elderly*. Lexington, Mass.: Lexington Books, 1976.

Goldsmith, J. & Goldsmith, S. *Crime and the elderly*. Lexington, Mass.: D.C. Heath, 1976.

Goldsmith, J. & Tomas, N.E. Crimes against the elderly: A continuing national crisis. *Aging*, 1974, *236*, 10-13.

Graham, V. Crime haunts urban elderly. *Syracuse Herald-Journal*, March 23, 1977, 1.

Greenstein, M. Fear and nonreporting by elders: An invitation to law enforcement. *Police Chief*, 1977, *44*, 46-47.

Gross, P. Summary report: Crime, safety, and the senior citizen. *Police Chief*, 1977, *44*, 18-26.

Harris, L. *The myth and reality of aging in America*, The National Council on Aging, Washington, D.C., 1975.

Hindelang, M. *An analysis of victimization survey results from the eight impact cities*, USGPO, Washington, D.C., 1976.

Kelley, C. *Crime in the United States, 1975*, USGPO, Washington, D.C., 1975.

Kimmel, D.C. *Adulthood and aging*. New York: John Wiley, 1974.

Lawton, M.P., Nahemow, L., Yaffee, S. & Feldman, S. Psychological aspects of crime and fear of crime. In J. Goldsmith & S. Goldsmith (Eds.), *Crime and the elderly*. Lexington, Mass.: Lexington Books, 1976.

Lebowitz, B.D. Age and fearfulness: Personal and situational factors. *Journal of Gerontology*, 1975, *30*, 696-700.

Maddox, G.L. Fact and artifact: Evidence bearing on disengagement theory from the Duke Geriatrics Project. *Human Development*, 1965, *8*, 117-130.

Mauss, A.L. *Social problems as social movements*. Philadelphia: Lippincott, 1975.

Neugarten, B. Personality and aging. In J.E. Birren & K.W. Schaie (Eds.), *Handbook of the psychology of aging*. New York: Van Nostrand Reinhold, 1977.

Patterson, A. Environmental indicators. *Police Chief*, 1977, *44*, 42-45.

Pope, C.E. & Fayerherm, W. The effects of crime on the elderly. *Police Chief*, 1976, *43*, 48-51.

Riley, M.W. & Foner, A. *Aging and society, Vol. 1*. New York: Russell Sage, 1968.

Riley, M.W. & Waring, J. Age and aging. In Robert K. Merton & R. Nisbet (Eds.) *Contemporary social problems*. New York: Harcourt Brace Jovanovich, 1976.

Schultz, J.H. Income distribution and the aging. In R.H. Binstock & E. Shanas (Eds.) *Handbook of aging and the social sciences*. New York: Van Nostrand Reinhold, 1976.

Shanas, E. Measuring the home health needs of the aged in five countries. *Journal of Gerontology*, 1971, *26*, 37-40.

Shanas, E. & Maddox, G.L. Aging, health, and the organization of health resources. In R.N. Binstock & E. Shanas (Eds.) *Handbook of aging and the social sciences*. New York: Van Nostrand Reinhold, 1976.

Sherman, E.A., Newman, E.S. & Nelson, A.D. Patterns of age integration in public housing and the incidence and fears of crime among elderly tenants. In J. Goldsmith & S. Goldsmith (Eds.) *Crime and the elderly*. Lexington, Mass.: D.C. Heath, 1976.

Sicker, M. A public perspective: The elderly and the criminal justice system. *Police Chief*, 1977, *44*, 38-41.

Streib, G.F. Social stratification and aging. In R.N. Binstock & E. Shanas (Eds.) *Handbook of aging and the social sciences*. New York: Van Nostrand Reinhold, 1976.

Sundeen, R.A. & Mathieu, J.T. The fear of crime and its consequences among the elderly in three urban communities. *Gerontologist*, 1975, *16*, 211-219.

Sykes, R. The urban police function in regard to the elderly: A special case of police community relations. In J. Goldsmith & S. Goldsmith (Eds.) *Crime and the elderly*. Lexington, Mass.: Lexington Books, 1976.

Tighe, J. Survey of crimes against the elderly. *Police Chief*, 1977, *44*, 30-33.

U.S. Bureau of the Census. *Demographic aspects of aging and the older population in the United States*, USGPO, Washington, D.C., 1976.

Weiss, C. *Evaluation research*. Englewood Cliffs, N.J.: Prentice-Hall, 1972.

Wolf, R. Senior citizen survey: An aid to designing prevention programs. *Police Chief*, 1977, *44*, 27-29.

Younger, E.J. The California experience in crime prevention programs with senior citizens. In J. Goldsmith & S. Goldsmith (Eds.) *Crime and the elderly*. Lexington, Mass.: Lexington Books, 1976.

3 Minority Elderly
Valaida Littlejohn Wise
William J. Hoyer

Black Americans are four times as likely to be burglarized and twice as likely to be assaulted as whites. Black women are four times as likely to be raped as white women. Crime rates against minorities are higher, and are increasing at a faster rate, than against whites. According to recent Law Enforcement Assistance Administration (LEAA) statistics, there has been a 64% increase in minor assaults and a 30% increase in aggravated assaults of black women since 1976. How do these high rates of crime affect minority elderly? The purpose of this chapter is to review the victimization problem as it affects the nonwhite aged, and to discuss implications for police-community relations and police training. Special attention is given to factors which account for the increased vulnerability of minority elderly.

One factor associated with vulnerability is life expectancy, and there is an ethnic difference in life expectancy; on the average whites live seven years longer than blacks. This difference may be related to several factors, including a generally lower socioeconomic status and emotional and psychological effects fostered by years of racial oppression. Although, on the average, whites outlive blacks, the situation appears to reverse itself for blacks who are "survivors"; that is, at age 75 there is an increase in survival rates among black elderly (Butler & Lewis, 1977). However, proportionately, twice as many whites reach the age of 75. This finding is consistent with a higher incidence of poor health among blacks who often do not have access to adequate medical care. In the 1970 census blacks constituted 11.2% of the total United States population, but only 7.8% of the total elderly population. There are now approximately 1.7 million elderly black Americans, and this number has steadily increased; in 1960 there were 1.2 million, and in 1970 there were 1.6 million. These statistics point to a greater rate of growth in the black elderly population than in the total black population. In 1975, 7% of America's blacks were age 65 or over, as compared to 6.2% in 1960. As in the white elderly population, women outnumber men, and the ratio of women to men increases with advancing years. In 1960, for example, there were 115 women per 100 men who were black elderly; in 1970 the ratio was 131 women per 100 men. Although the ratio of women to men is slightly larger for blacks than whites in the general population regardless of age, this sex differential for the 65 or over blacks is not quite as large as it is for white elderly.

On the average there are broad diferences in the socioeconomic level and living arrangements of nonwhite and white elderly (Dancy, 1977). There are relatively few minority elderly who are well off economically. Depending on how the poverty level is defined, between 37% and 70% of the black elderly live below, or near, the poverty level. Regardless of which income level cut-off is used for tabulation, there are over twice as many poor black elderly as there are poor white elderly. Atchley (1977) attributes the greater poverty of minority elderly to past job discrimination. Proportionately greater numbers of elderly blacks than whites receive the minimum Social Security benefit. The pensions of blacks average $250 less per year than the pensions of whites.

The four states with the highest proportion of blacks in the elderly poor population are District of Columbia, 64%; Mississippi, 49.2%; South Carolina, 43.1%; and Louisiana, 42%.

America's black population appears to be highly concentrated geographically. The largest concentration of elderly blacks is in the South—61%—and in California, New York, Pennsylvania, Texas, and Illinois. Over 25% of the older black population live in Texas, New York, Louisiana, and Georgia, and 55.8% live in ten states.

Because of the rural to urban migration throughout this century, and the more recent urban to suburban trend in the United States, elderly blacks are concentrated in the central cities, usually in the oldest, poorest housing. In the rural South the living arrangements are likely to be equally dismal. "If you are black and live in a southern state your chances are 41 out of 100 of lacking one or more basic plumbing facilities" (Lawton, 1977).

One consequence of a lifetime of economic and social deprivation is reflected in educational level differences between elderly blacks and whites. According to 1970 Census Bureau data, blacks between the ages of 65 and 74 completed 6.1 years of education, while whites completed 8.9 years; for those over 75, the figures are 5.2 and 6.1 for blacks and whites, respectively. It is interesting to note that elderly black women, who averaged 6.8 years, are more educated than elderly black men, who averaged 5.1 years, suggesting that men were often forced to leave school to work (Kent, 1970).

Police officers who work in the black community are likely to encounter disputes and fights among family members. Ploski and Brown (1967) have discussed the history of this problem. There is little need to document the negative effects of slavery on the black family unit; however, even following the Reconstruction period after the Civil War, economic conditions interfered with the development of a stable black family. As Kent (1970) pointed out, the result has been a pattern of family disorganization which has particularly affected the elderly. Compared to whites, separation, desertion, and divorce rates are higher, and there is a greater incidence of illegitimate births.

Most of today's older blacks were born before 1910 and grew into young adults during an era in which police brutality, racial oppression, and discrimination were the norm. As children, they frequently witnessed or received physical abuse at the hands of white police officers. Therefore, many of them fear and mistrust the police and the entire law enforcement system. During the 50s and 60s The Kerner Commission substantiated the pervasiveness of alienation between the police and the black community. This alienation not only involved the youth of the black community, but the elderly as well; and it included not only the cop on the beat, but often the total criminal justice system. There is little or no history of fair law enforcement to which elderly blacks can relate. On the contrary, there is a widespread opinion that little effort is expended on the apprehension of criminals and that criminal acts have been tacitly sanctioned. A predominate view of blacks is that there is a double standard of law enforcement and justice, and this attitude serves to heighten feelings of isolation and alienation. Elderly blacks even seem to be ambivalent about black policemen, often regarding them as part of the oppressive establishment. Because of this feeling of ambivalence elderly black have no one on whom they can rely in times of trouble. Moreover, their alienation and fear make it less than likely that they will report crimes they have witnessed or ones in which they were victimized. Elderly blacks frequently would rather pretend it didn't happen than contact the police. These fears are particularly deep-rooted, and cannot be easily alleviated; but they should not be neglected.

It is difficult to get an accurate image of America's elderly blacks. Some statistics have been presented; but, if we are to understand the position of the aged black, both information and experience are necessary. In 1896 W.E.B. DuBois conducted a study of the Negroes in Philadelphia, and in 1899 the results were published in *The Philadelphia Negro*. Many of his observations still apply to today's minority urbanites.

> In Philadelphia as elsewhere in the United States, the existence of certain peculiar social problems affecting the Negro people are plainly manifest. Here is a large group

of people—perhaps forty-five thousand, a city within a city—who do not form an integral part of the larger social group. This in itself is not altogether unusual; there are other unassimilated groups; Jews, Italians, even Americans; and yet in the case of the Negroes the segregation is more conspicuous, more patent to the eye, and so intertwined with a long historic evolution, with peculiarly pressing social problems of poverty, ignorance, crime and labor, that the Negro problem far surpasses in scientific interest and social gravity, most of the other race or class questions.

SPANISH-AMERICAN ELDERLY

The second largest ethnic minority in the United States is the Spanish-American population. Persons of Spanish origin include Central and South Americans, Cubans, Mexicans, and Puerto Ricans, and other Spanish-speaking people. In March, 1976 the Bureau of the Census estimated that there were 6,590,000 Mexicans, 1,753,000 Puerto Ricans, 752,000 Central and South Americans, 687,000 Cubans, and 1,335,000 other Spanish-speaking people living in the United States.

Mexican-Americans, the largest Spanish group, live mainly in urban areas in the five southwestern states of Arizona, California, Colorado, New Mexico, and Texas. Only about 4% of the total Spanish population is elderly, compared to 10% of the total American population. New Mexico has the highest proportion of Spanish-speaking persons in its elderly poor population. Nationally, approximately 33% of the 375,000 Spanish-speaking older persons in the United States live in poverty; that percentage for the state of New Mexico is 45.2%. The average life expectancy is approximately 57 years, which is much lower than the average for both whites and blacks. Elderly Spanish-Americans experience poverty, inadequate medical care, poor housing, and few educational opportunities.

The shortened life expectancy of the Spanish-American population can also be understood in terms of a "youthful" age distribution. The median age of Spanish-Americans is 20.9, compared to almost 30 for the general population; and about 13% are under age 5, compared to 7% for the general population. Unfortunately, the data are unclear as to the degree of increased mortality attributable to minority status.

Individuals of Spanish descent often prefer to reside in neighborhoods where there is a commonality of language, background, and culture. In New York City, for example, Puerto Ricans are concentrated in Spanish Harlem, an ethnic ghetto. Important aspects of police work in the area are an ability to communicate in Spanish and an understanding of cultural patterns. Many Puerto Ricans, however, regardless of age, view the officer as a representative of an inequitable system. He is either too oppressive or he fails to provide help and protection; he is either too personal or too distant and aloof. These attitudes are especially strong in the elderly Spanish and they serve to interfere with effective police work.

MINORITY FEARS

While many of the problems of the minority elderly are similar to those of the white elderly, the problems are " . . . exaggerated and compounded by a more deeply embedded and concentrated poverty, as well as by other factors such as racial discrimination" (Jackson, 1971). Two areas that are especially problematic for minority elderly are fear of crime and fear of the police. There are data showing that blacks are more fearful of crime than are whites (Hindelang, 1976). Braungart, Braungart, and Hoyer (1978), in their analysis of a national probability sample consisting of 1499 cases (NORC data, 1976), found that 70% of the blacks over 60 expressed fear of walking in their neighborhoods, compared to 49% for whites. Blacks between the ages of 18 and 29 expressed little fear, but 79% of the middle-aged black women and 28% of the middle-aged black men expressed fear of crime (Table 3.1).

In addition to a greater fear of crime on the part of the minority elderly, there is ironically also a greater fear of police. For a long time black people have viewed the police uniform and the police station as symbols of oppression. Before the civil rights movement of the early 1960s southern blacks were sometimes beaten and killed by white police, who had little, if any, special training in crowd control. Racial prejudice often prohibited the fair treatment of blacks by the law enforcement system, and this, in turn, has contributed to the negative attitude of many members of the black community toward the police. Typically, white policemen had contact only with minority individuals who were suspected or convicted of a crime and who often supported minority stereotypes.

Some of the views of the minority elderly toward the law enforcement system are reflected in these statements: "If you are a witness to a crime, you'll get beaten up. It's best to keep out of it"; "They will not even catch the offender, so why bother reporting the crime"; "The offender, if caught, will get

Table 3.1 Percentage Fearful by Age and Race

	Race							
	White				Black			
Age Group	Men	Total	Women	Total	Men	Total	Women	Total
Young Adult	21%	(168)	64%	(178)	6%	(17)	38%	(21)
Middle Aged	20%	(279)	58%	(375)	28%	(29)	79%	(28)
Elderly	29%	(149)	63%	(201)	59%	(17)	81%	(16)

Data from the National Opinion Survey Research Center (1976); see Braungart, Braungart, & Hoyer (1978).

you after he's back on the streets"; and "The offender's gang will get even with you."

Blacks and whites often differ in their views of police. Hadar and Snortum (1975) found that 202 community residents and 53 policemen agreed on standards for police conduct, but disagreed sharply in their views of actual police behavior. Women, whites, and older people set the most rigorous standards, and men, minorities, and youth were most dissatisfied with police practices.

POLICE-COMMUNITY RELATIONS

One of the major issues of concern in American society is the quality of law enforcement. Police represent the narrow blue line between anarchy and order. In a country that has grown so rapidly and that has had a history of immigration and slavery it is obvious that issues related to the quality of law enforcement depend on *whose* laws and orders are being enforced. Although most police think of themselves as crime fighters, approximately 80% of the police officer's time is spent providing a wide variety of community services, such as handling traffic accidents, giving directions, and resolving—or trying to resolve—family disputes. Crime-related activities take up less than 20% of the average police officer's on-duty time. Thus, the police officer who enforces order in the black community should be very familiar with the attitudes and values of that community in order to be maximally effective.

It is often thought that different police chiefs and departments set somewhat different priorities and standards for the officer's conduct on the street. Perhaps the burden of maintaining communication with the community should be on the department and its leadership. Policemen experience alienation, rejection, and hostility in a job involving danger, threat, and authority. To develop ways whereby alienation could be reduced through increased communication and cooperation with citizens should be a high priority for all police.

While elderly blacks experience difficulty in dealing with and relating to police officers, the officers have difficulty relating to the black elderly; it must be recognized that communication is a two-way street. Most police officers are themselves white and nonelderly and, therefore, it is difficult for them to put themselves into the position of someone who is their antithesis. The police officer is sometimes uncomfortable, and this feeling is subtly conveyed to the older person. In other words, unfamiliarity leads to fear and apprehension for both the elderly person and the officer.

Police officers may be generally unfamiliar with the black family system and the black community. For example, those who are not familiar with the black community may not fully realize or understand the special significance of the church to elderly blacks (Kent, 1971). Police work in black neighborhoods is especially difficult when the age factor is added; an elderly victim may know who committed the crime, but may not want to turn in the offender to the police. Moreover a large percentage of elderly blacks are originally from the South and have speech and language patterns, as well as value systems, that are unfamiliar to the northern urban policeman. The police officer's inability to overcome barriers of communication with elderly minority individuals may be perceived as disrespectful. Because of differences in heritage and culture, police officers may be violating basic traditions and interpersonal styles unknowingly. Acceptance, empathy, and understanding are important characteristics for effective police work; in fact, a white person's familiarity with blacks and black culture will aid acceptance, empathy, and understanding in any setting (Jones & Seagull, 1977).

Understanding the ways in which minorities in American society have been oppressed and denied equal opportunity is helpful to effective police work. Whenever possible, the officer should consider which actions will lead to a constructive interchange and resolution, and thereby reduce the elderly citizens' feelings of oppression and discrimination.

Goldsmith (1976) and others have discussed the shift from crime-centered law enforcement to full-service policing. Traditionally, police work has been seen as crime control, investigation, and the apprehending of criminals. The full-service approach emphasizes police-community relations. In addition to dealing with crime, the full-service officer involves himself in many types of noncrime situations, ranging from assisting a child who has lost a pet to rescuing an elderly person stranded by a snowstorm or other natural disaster.

The trend toward full-service policing must gather more momentum in order to strengthen police-community relations in minority neighborhoods. However, there are very few visible incentives for improving police-community relations in minority neighborhoods. The police officer's job expectations are to catch criminals and enforce laws; his success in these tasks leads to the greatest rewards, peer respect, and promotions (Goldsmith, 1976). The community relations work, which takes up most of the officer's on-duty time, often goes unrecognized and unrewarded, and may even be devalued by fellow officers.

The full-service concept would provide official recognition for the importance of the 80-90 percent of the officer's job which constitutes service rather than law enforcement functions. This could improve the officer's appreciation for the breadth of police functions both explicit and implicit (Mintz & Sandler, 1974).

Strengthening police-community relations should be considered the task of *all* police officers rather than of those few who have been specifically appointed for this purpose. Incentives and training in the area of police-community relations need to be provided for all officers. "We need to *legitimize* how most officers spend most of their time" (Goldsmith, 1976).

How does the police officer "break into" the minority community? Basically this is a question of how friendship and trust can develop in interpersonal relationships. Time, a sincere concern for the other's welfare, and honesty are clearly some of the ingredients.

REFERENCES

Atchley, R.C. *The social forces in later life*. Belmont, Cal.: Wadsworth, 1977.

Braungart, M.M., Braungart, R.G., & Hoyer, W.J. Age, sex, and social factors in fear of crime. Paper presented at the meeting of the Southern Sociological Society, New Orleans, 1978.

Butler, R.N. *Why survive? Being old in America*. New York: Harper & Row, 1975.

Butler, R.N., & Lewis, M.I. *Aging and mental health: Positive psychosocial approaches*. St. Louis: Mosby, 1977.

Dancy, J. *The black elderly. A guide for practitioners*. Ann Arbor, Mich.: Institute of Gerontology, University of Michigan-Wayne State University, 1977.

DuBois, W.E.B. *The Philadelphia Negro*. First published in 1899, reissued in 1967 by Benjamin Bloom, Inc., New York.

Goldsmith, J. Police and the older victim: Keys to a changing perspective. *Police Chief*, 1976, *43*, 19-23.

Hadar, I., & Snortum, J.R. The eye of the beholder: Differential perceptions of police by the police and the public. *Criminal Justice and Behavior*, 1975, *2*, 37-54.

Hindelang, M. An analysis of victimization survey results from the eight impact cities. U.S.G.P.O., Washington, D.C. 1976.

Jackson, H.C. National caucus on the black aged: A progress report. *Aging and Human Development*, 1971, *3*, 226-231.

Jones, A., & Seagull, A.A. Dimensions of the relationship between the black client and the white therapist: A theoretical overview. *American Psychologist*, 1977, *32*, 850-855.

Kent, D.P. The negro aged. *The Gerontologist*, 1971, *11*, 48-51.

Lawton, M.P. *Planning and managing housing for the elderly*. New York: Wiley, 1977.

Mintz, E., & Sandler, G.B. Instituting a full-service orientation to policing. *The Police Chief*, 1974, *42*, 50.

Ploski, H.A. & Brown, R.E., Jr. (Eds.) *The negro almanac*. New York: Bellwether Publishing Co., 1967.

4 Crime Prevention and the Elderly
Philip J. Gross

As crime continues to plague communities across the country, elderly citizens are working with law enforcement agencies to do their share in local crime prevention programs. At the same time, the law enforcement community has recognized both the special needs of the elderly and, equally as important, the positive impact senior citizens can have on a department's crime prevention efforts. The partnership of these two groups is important because, as our birth-rate decreases, the number of senior citizens will not only increase but senior citizens will increasingly represent the public that law enforcers are sworn to "serve and protect." Therefore, law enforcement administrators, in conjunction with the appropriate community agencies, must determine how law enforcement operations and crime prevention efforts can best be directed to better serve this segment of our society.

Currently, the relationship between crime and the elderly is open to question. Crime statistics generally are not broken down by age. While most police departments have youth officers, few have senior citizen officers, although this situation is changing. Senior volunteers serve in some law enforcement agencies, while

Except where otherwise noted, the materials contained herein are adapted from the findings of a national Model Project on Aging funded by the Administration on Aging, U.S. Department of Health, Education and Welfare (Grant Number 90-A-494/01) to the Technical Research Services Divisions of the International Association of Chiefs of Police. The author served as the Project Manager for this study.

other agencies have developed crime prevention programs aimed at the special needs of elderly. However, these practices are neither widespread nor uniform.

To develop a base of information concerning the current relationship between crime, the elderly and law enforcement, the International Association of Chiefs of Police (IACP) surveyed 500 law enforcement agencies in an attempt to identify the links between the three. This 1976 survey was answered by 180, or 36% of the agencies polled. A summary of their responses provides valuable information and insights. A careful review of the findings should help an individual department or officer to assess current or potential relationships with senior citizens.

SURVEY FINDINGS

The first part of the survey dealt with voluntary employment opportunities for retired individuals within law enforcement agencies. The survey returns indicated that 10% of the responding departments operated programs in which senior citizen volunteers were used to replace or assist sworn personnel performing nonhazardous police assignments.

Table 4.1 lists the number of departments operating or planning to operate volunteer programs, divides the volunteers into senior and nonsenior categories, and pinpoints those areas where it was felt that there was potential for senior citizen involvement. (There may be some discrepancy of column totals in the tables due to inconsistency in form completion.)

In addition to the use of senior volunteers, the survey was concerned with the victimization of the elderly and crime prevention programs designed to deal with their problems. The different crime prevention programs that have been implemented for senior citizens during the past five years are illustrated in Table 4.2. Those departments which perceived a need for additional crime prevention programs—124, or 69%, of the responding departments—were asked to list the five most important areas in which crime prevention programs are needed. The responses to these questions are presented in Table 4.3.

The last area of the survey involved the problems patrol and investigative personnel encountered in dealing with senior citizens. Table 4.4 contains a list of the problems posed and the agency responses. Reviewing these responses in conjunction with the information provided in the following section gives a better insight into the sources of many of these responses.

In trying to assess the involvement of community organizations in crime prevention programs for the elderly, the survey asked about groups other than the police that were undertaking the same kind of task. Over 50% of the responding departments stated that other groups or agencies provided crime prevention programs for senior citizens; these included 61 retirement clubs, 53 local or county social service agencies, 42 service clubs or organizations, and 38

Table 4.1 Current Volunteer Programs in Law Enforcement Agencies

Job Classification	Planned or Proposed	In Operation	Non-Senior Volunteer	Senior Volunteer	Potential for Senior Citizen Involvement
Internal Administration:					
Personal matters	0 (0%)	1 (1%)	4 (2%)	1 (1%)	18 (10%)
Budget preparation	0 (0%)	1 (1%)	3 (2%)	0 (0%)	21 (12%)
Budget control/acctg.	0 (0%)	0 (0%)	2 (1%)	0 (0%)	13 (7%)
Data Processing	0 (0%)	1 (1%)	3 (2%)	0 (0%)	22 (12%)
Planning and research	1 (1%)	2 (1%)	4 (2%)	1 (1%)	28 (16%)
Legal	2 (1%)	2 (1%)	7 (4%)	0 (0%)	26 (14%)
Training	1 (1%)	1 (1%)	4 (2%)	1 (1%)	36 (20%)
Clerical	3 (2%)	5 (3%)	11 (6%)	2 (1%)	68 (38%)
Other	0 (0%)	2 (1%)	5 (3%)	1 (1%)	6 (3%)
Internal Operations:					
Dispatching	1 (1%)	5 (3%)	7 (4%)	0 (0%)	23 (13%)
Emergency operations	0 (0%)	16 (9%)	15 (8%)	4 (2%)	17 (9%)
Booking	1 (1%)	3 (2%)	8 (4%)	2 (1%)	10 (6%)
Arrestee counseling	0 (0%)	4 (2%)	6 (3%)	3 (2%)	22 (12%)
Crime victim counseling	4 (2%)	9 (5%)	10 (6%)	7 (4%)	55 (31%)
Equipment maintenance	1 (0%)	4 (2%)	6 (3%)	0 (0%)	38 (21%)
Criminalistics	0 (0%)	1 (1%)	2 (1%)	1 (1%)	13 (7%)
Property control	0 (0%)	1 (1%)	3 (2%)	2 (1%)	42 (23%)
Other	0 (0%)	12 (7%)	10 (6%)	2 (1%)	2 (1%)
External Operations:					
Traffic control	1 (1%)	32 (18%)	30 (17%)	6 (3%)	22 (12%)
Bicycle registration	6 (3%)	13 (7%)	13 (7%)	5 (3%)	91 (51%)
Operation identification	9 (5%)	28 (16%)	24 (13%)	14 (8%)	107 (59%)
Anti-burglary programs	10 (6%)	29 (16%)	23 (13%)	15 (8%)	94 (52%)
Anti-fraud programs	6 (3%)	9 (5%)	9 (5%)	6 (3%)	87 (49%)
Self-defense programs	2 (1%)	10 (6%)	11 (6%)	5 (3%)	35 (19%)
Check-cashing programs	3 (2%)	7 (4%)	7 (4%)	3 (2%)	74 (41%)
Other	4 (2%)	25 (14%)	26 (14%)	14 (8%)	12 (7%)
Patrol					8 (4%)

From *The Police Chief*, p. 10, February 1976. Reprinted by permission.

religious groups. There were also 33 other groups involving, but not limited to, state agencies, financial institutions, and the news media. These responses clearly indicate that many communities are aware of the need in this area and are actively doing something to cope with the problem of crime and the elderly.

Table 4.2 Crime Prevention Programs Implemented for Senior Citizens

Type of Program	Departments Involved	
Operation identification	125	(69%)
Self-defense programs	63	(35%)
Residential security	120	(67%)
Business security	77	(43%)
Anti-purse snatching/ pocket picking	96	(53%)
Anti-fraud programs	91	(51%)
Mailbox security	42	(23%)
Check-cashing programs	46	(26%)
Other	15	(8%)
None	19	(11%)

From *The Police Chief*, p. 10, February 1976. Reprinted by permission.

Table 4.3 Senior Citizen Victimization and its Prevention

Crime	Most Frequent Crime Victims		Crime Prevention Programs Needed	
Forcible rape	2	(1%)	6	(3%)
Robbery	66	(37%)	58	(32%)
Aggravated assault	20	(11%)	15	(8%)
Burglary	122	(68%)	102	(57%)
Pocket picking or purse snatching	129	72%)	99	(55%)
Theft of income checks (i.e. Social Security, welfare, etc.)	99	(55%)	73	(41%)
Theft of motor vehicle	8	(4%)	5	(3%)
Theft of recreational equipment or bicycles	6	(3%)	5	(3%)
Theft from motor vehicle	21	(12%)	16	(9%)
Confidence games and deceptive practices	150	(83%)	104	(58%)
Embezzlement	17	(9%)	16	(9%)
Intimidation	27	(15%)	14	(8%)
Telephone harassment	32	(18%)	23	(13%)
Vandalism	99	(55%)	56	(31%)
Arson	0	(0%)	2	(1%)
Other	5	(3%)	8	(4%)

From *The Police Chief*, p. 11, February 1976. Reprinted by permission.

Table 4.4 Problems Between the Police and the Senior Citizen

Problems	Agencies	
A. Calls for service which seem to be a result of imaginary problems	101	(56%)
B. Calls for service which appear to be a result of loneliness rather than the need for assistance	88	(49%)
C. Calls from "chronic complainers"	116	(64%)
D. Communication problems resulting from physical handicaps such as sight and hearing difficulties	40	(22%)
E. Communication problems because of language barriers	18	(10%)
F. Officer's lack of understanding of the problems faced by the elderly	77	(43%)
G. Elderly's lack of understanding of the police role and the scope of service	121	(67%)
H. Unnecessary and bothersome calls resulting from senior citizen monitoring of police radio	8	(4%)
I. Other	20	(12%)

From *The Police Chief*, p. 11, February 1976. Reprinted by permission.

THE OLDER VICTIM*

While senior citizens are the victims of the same types of crimes as younger individuals, crime tends to have a more profound and lasting effect on the older victim than on the younger one. The elderly victim should be viewed as a special and distinctive case for a number of reasons.

1. The elderly usually have a reduced or low income. Thus, the impact of any loss of economic resources is relatively great.

2. Older people are more likely to be victimized time and again, often by the same offender.

3. Older people are more likely to live alone, and social isolation increases vulnerability to crime.

4. Older people are weaker physically and have less stamina. Therefore, they are less able to defend themselves, less able to escape from threatening situations, and less able to resist attackers. They are also far more likely to suffer from physical ailments, such as loss of hearing or sight, arthritis, and circulatory problems, which further increase their vulnerability.

---

*Jack Goldsmith, "Police and the Older Victim: Keys to a Changing Perspective," *The Police Chief*, February, 1976, p. 19 and Jack Goldsmith and Noel E. Tomas, "Crimes Against the Elderly: A Continuing National Crisis," *Aging*, June-July 1974, p. 236-237.

5. Criminals, aware of this fragile physical condition and, thus, the vulnerability, are more likely to seek out an elderly target.

6. Older people are more likely to live in high crime neighborhoods as a result of diminished income and of being rooted in central cities. Thus, they find themselves living among the group most likely to victimize them—the unemployed, teen-age dropouts.

7. The dates when monthly pension and benefit checks are received, and hence the dates when older people are most likely to have cash on their person or in their homes, are widely known.

8. For physical, financial, or other reasons, older people are less likely to drive or own a private automobile. They depend on walking or on public transportation.

9. Older people are particularly susceptible to fraud and confidence games.

10. Older people most often fall victim to the crime of personal larceny with contact, the theft of purse, wallet, or cash taken directly from the person of the victim.

11. Older people are aware of their increased vulnerability to criminal behavior, and this awareness often has a chilling effect upon their freedom of movement. Fear of victimization may cause self-imposed "house arrest" among older people. Even in situations where the fear of being victimized may be exaggerated or unwarranted, the effect on the older persons can be just as severe as when the fears are justified.

12. Because the American culture associates loss of status and decreased sense of personal efficacy with being old, older people may be less likely to process complaints through the criminal justice bureaucracy and to draw upon available community resources for protection and redress.

In order for law enforcement agencies to focus effectively on the elderly victim, it is imperative that they recognize these several ways in which there may be a distinctive impact of crime on the elderly.

CRIME PREVENTION PROGRAMMING FOR THE ELDERLY

Careful planning must precede the implementation of a new crime prevention program for senior citizens. To ensure that new efforts respond to the needs of the community's senior citizens, the planning process should include input from the local or state Office on Aging, from members of the senior community, and from other appropriate community organizations—such as representatives from a local university's gerontology program. This group effort will help to avoid the pitfalls common to those programs which are designed in accordance with the needs as perceived by the police rather than in accordance with the needs as perceived by the elderly.

Crime prevention programs should be developed with the following points in mind: the police alone cannot control crime; citizen participation in crime prevention efforts is essential to preventing crime; and, if given the opportunity, senior citizens have the desire and ability to work with law enforcement agencies in developing and implementing programs to make their communities a safer place in which to live.

Program Planning

An initial step in developing a senior citizen crime prevention program is the preparation of a plan of action designed to ensure the orderly progress of the program's design and implementation. A model program plan (Table 4.5) was

Table 4.5 Model Program Plan

I. *Problem Identification*. Identify the problem and define the task to be performed.
   A. Data collection
      1. Determine the type or kind of data required.
      2. Select the time frame for which the data will be collected.
      3. Collect the available data from police incident reports and other available crime statistics or information sources.
      4. Evaluate the available data to determine additional data requirements.
      5. Collect the additional data required.
   B. Data analysis
      1. Organize the data collected.
      2. Analyze the data in terms of the victim, offender, type of crime, time of crime, and location of crime, taking into consideration the location of the occurrence and its relation to the victim's and offender's residence, if deemed appropriate.
II. *Available resources*
   A. Identify those community agencies, organizations, and individuals who may be able to provide input.
   B. Identify those personnel within the law enforcement agency who would be valuable assets to this program.
   C. After consultation with these agencies, determine which individuals should be invited to participate in the program planning.
III. *Program selection*
   A. List all possible or feasible programs which are felt to have a potential impact on the problem as defined in the first step of this outline.
   B. Assess the program alternatives considering all positive and negative factors of each.
   C. Based upon the assessment, select the most feasible alternative for implementation.
IV. *Program implementation*
   A. Design policy and establish those procedures required for the implementation of the chosen program.
   B. Assign responsibilities for implementing the program to the appropriate personnel.
   C. Implement the program as designed.
V. *Program evaluation*
   A. Determine, prior to program implementation, the methods to be used to evaluate the program.
   B. Conduct the evaluation in accordance with the predetermined methodology.
   C. Based upon the evaluation, review the program as it now operates and make those changes as deemed necessary.

From *The Police Chief*, p. 12, February 1976. Reprinted by permission.

developed by the IACP for use during its project, Crime, Safety and the Senior Citizen. The following details of the plan are discussed as examples of points to consider in adapting the model plan to local senior citizen programs.

Prior to collecting data concerning crime and the elderly, certain parameters must be established to limit the collection to that information actually needed. One basic consideration in defining parameters for reviewing crime data involves designating the age of the population to be studied. Since there is no nationwide age definition for senior citizens, local social service agencies should be consulted. Consideration also has to be given to the geographic area to be covered, the length of time to be reviewed, and the type or types of offenses to be considered. In addition to police reports, data may be obtained through victim interviews, census reports, or studies done by agencies responsible for services to the aging.

Analysis of the data should basically answer six questions. *Who* are the victim and the perpetrator? *What* crime occurred and what were the individuals doing that may have precipitated the event? *Where* did the crime occur as to specific location and in reference to the residence of the victim and suspect? *When* did the crime take place—time of day, day of the week, and month of the year? *Why* did the suspect commit the offense, and why was the particular victim selected? *How* was the act committed?

With this information available, planning can proceed to develop programs describing countermeasures to those acts which precipitated the crime. Although preventive or deterrent action could be aimed at either the victim or the offender, the chances are greater that the victim will more readily participate. Elderly citizens can be taught such preventive steps as:

Always stay alert to your surroundings;

Carry money inconspicuously and carry as little of it as possible;

Choose the busiest and best-lit streets, and try to go out with a companion;

Don't leave your purse unattended while shopping;

Don't carry a purse if you don't need to;

Avoid alleys and sparsely-travelled areas;

Have your key ready when you get to your door;

If a stranger comes to your door, ask him for identification;

Always report a crime, no matter how insignificant you think it is; and above all,

Don't resist! Give the robber what he wants; be calm and attentive.

Most burglars enter a residence through a door. Police officers generally find that between 25% and 30% of the homes in burglary-prone neighborhoods are unlocked. There are many steps that elderly homeowners and apartment dwellers can take to reduce the chances of burglary.

Always lock your doors, and have effective door locks installed.

Keep your "hidden key" in a hidden place.

Be wary of unsolicited phone calls and "wrong numbers."

Don't keep large amounts of money and valuables in predictable and accessible places.

Leave a light and maybe a radio on while you're away for short periods.

Separate your house keys and car keys when leaving your auto in a public garage or at a service station.

When you are away for a long period, discontinue mail, dairy, newspaper, and other deliveries.

Don't notify burglars by putting social notes of your trip in the newspaper. Wait until after you return to tell everyone about the trip.

Mark your valuable property.

Have your lawn tended and put lights on timers while you are away.

Set up a neighborhood security watch.

The Senior Citizen Survey

To assist local law enforcement agencies in assessing the attitudes and problems of local seniors in relation to their fears of crime, the effect of crime on the seniors' lifestyle, and those crime prevention measures currently being practiced by the seniors, the IACP developed a Crime and the Senior Citizen survey (Fig. 4.1). This version of the survey was based on the experiences of the project's demonstration sites: Miami Beach, Florida; Omaha, Nebraska; Jersey City, New Jersey; Syracuse, New York; and Mansfield, Ohio. The survey was designed to be used in a number of ways. The Omaha Police Division gave the survey to volunteers attending crime prevention programs while the Miami Beach Police Department used members of the Department's Explorer Post to canvas, on a door-to-door basis, those neighborhoods that reported crime statistics indicating problem or high crime areas for senior citizens.

Several benefits derive from using this survey in conjunction with reported crime statistics. For one, reported crime statistics are usually biased because they represent only crimes actually reported to the police. By using this survey, an administrator can approximate the percentage of seniors who actually report crime, the socioeconomic status of the seniors by neighborhood, and the effect crime has had on their daily activities. The survey can also serve as a means of opening communication between the police and senior citizens through the positive exchange resulting from using the survey. Through this interaction, officers can gather information concerning the fears of the elderly and can determine whether the fears expressed by the seniors actually correspond to reported crime statistics.

The manner in which the survey is administered must be considered in evaluating the responses. Because respondents may themselves bias the results, it is important to know whether it has been conducted in conjunction with crime prevention programs or gatherings other than door-to-door. For example, the fact that people were willing to travel to the meeting site may imply either that they were not afraid to leave their homes, or were terrified or interested enough

Fig. 4.1 Crime and the Senior Citizen

SECTION I. BACKGROUND INFORMATION

Your answers to the questions in this survey will help us in providing ways to protect all senior citizens.

Since these questions deal with background items, you may feel that you do not want to answer some of them. However, this entire questionnaire is strictly anonymous. There is no way you can be identified, so we hope you are willing to give accurate information.

Your answers may be very important in helping us solve the special problems of you and your fellow senior citizens.

1. Please give your age: ☐
2. Sex: ☐ Male ☐ Female
3. Living arrangements:
   - ☐ I live alone.
   - ☐ I live with 1 other person.
   - ☐ I live with 2 or more others.
4. Housing:
   - ☐ I own my own home.
   - ☐ I am renting my home.
   - ☐ I live with relatives.
   - ☐ Other.
5. Daily Activity:
   - ☐ I am self-sufficient for almost all routine household and shopping chores.
   - ☐ I have some help for these routine needs.
   - ☐ I have help for most of these needs.

SECTION II. GENERAL SURVEY

1. How often do you go out after dark?
   - ☐ 4 times a week or more
   - ☐ 1 to 3 times a week
   - ☐ 1 to 3 times a month
   - ☐ Less than once a month
   - ☐ Never
2. When do you feel safe in your home or apartment building?
   - ☐ Never ☐ Daytime
   - ☐ Nighttime ☐ Always
3. When do you feel safe in your yard or grounds of apartment?
   - ☐ Never ☐ Daytime
   - ☐ Nighttime ☐ Always

4. When do you feel safe in your neighborhood?
   - ☐ Never ☐ Daytime
   - ☐ Nighttime ☐ Always
5. When do you feel safe in the shopping areas you use?
   - ☐ Never ☐ Daytime
   - ☐ Nighttime ☐ Always
6. When do you feel safe on public transport?
   - ☐ Never ☐ Daytime
   - ☐ Nighttime ☐ Always
7. When do you feel safe in your car?
   - ☐ Never ☐ Daytime
   - ☐ Nighttime ☐ Always
8. Have you had contact with the police since living here?
   - ☐ No ☐ Yes, once
   - ☐ Yes, twice ☐ More than twice

   If you answered "No" to Question 8, go to Question 13.
9. If you said "Yes" to Question 8, what were the circumstances? Check *all* that apply:
   - ☐ I was the victim of a crime.
   - ☐ I was in an accident.
   - ☐ I was ill.
   - ☐ I needed other assistance.
   - ☐ Other. Explain: _____
10. If you answered Question 9, how would you describe the response time of the police?
    - ☐ Excellent ☐ Average ☐ Poor
11. If you answered Question 9, how would you describe the service provided by the police?
    - ☐ Excellent ☐ Average ☐ Poor
12. If you answered Question 9, how would you describe the overall service provided by other agencies involved?
    - ☐ Excellent ☐ Average ☐ Poor
    - ☐ What other agencies were involved?

    _____
    - ☐ No other agencies were involved
13. Have you ever attended a program presented by the police department?
    - ☐ Yes ☐ No
14. What was the subject discussed? _____
    - ☐ I do not remember.

Fig. 4.1 (continued)

15. Have you adopted crime prevention techniques as a result of the presentation? ☐ Yes ☐ No

16. If you *have not* had personal experience, how would you describe the police protection in your neighborhood?
    ☐ Excellent ☐ Average ☐ Poor
    ☐ I have had personal experience with the police

17. To what extent has your feeling about crime hampered your freedom of movement and activity throughout the city?
    ☐ Greatly ☐ Somewhat ☐ None

18. If you were alone in your home and felt afraid, who would you call *first*?
    ☐ Family   ☐ Neighbor
    ☐ Police   ☐ Security Guard
    ☐ Other. Explain: _____

19. Check each of the following things you usually do to protect yourself or your belongings:
    ☐ Hold onto my purse or pocketbook and don't put it down.
    ☐ Hide money in my home.
    ☐ Hide money on my person.
    ☐ Don't carry wallet or pocketbook.
    ☐ Carry only minimum amount of money necessary for purpose of my trip.
    ☐ Avoid going out at night.
    ☐ Avoid certain streets and areas.
    ☐ Go out with others, not alone.
    ☐ Avoid using public transportation.
    ☐ Have at home a lethal weapon (Gun, knife, etc.).
    ☐ Have at home a nonlethal weapon (Mace, alarm, etc.).
    ☐ Carry a lethal weapon.
    ☐ Carry a nonlethal weapon.
    ☐ Use special locks on my doors.
    ☐ Use special locks on my windows.
    ☐ Leave lights on.
    ☐ Use timer to switch lights on/off.
    ☐ Have my Social Security check mailed directly to bank.
    ☐ Other. Explain: _____
    _____
    ☐ None of the above.

SECTION III. VICTIMIZATION

1. How many times in the past 2 years have you been the victim of an offense?
   ☐ None ☐ 1 ☐ 2 ☐ 3
   ☐ More than 3

2. What kind(s) of offense(s) were they? (Check *all* that apply and circle the appropriate number of times for each.)

What Kind?		How Many?
☐ Disturbing the peace		1 2 3 More
☐ Assault		1 2 3 More
☐ Purse Snatch/ Pickpocket		1 2 3 More
☐ Theft of property		1 2 3 More
☐ Rape		1 2 3 More
☐ Fraud/Con Game		1 2 3 More
☐ Property destruction		1 2 3 More
☐ Theft from mailbox		1 2 3 More
☐ Other. Explain: _____		
☐ I have not been a victim.		

3. Think of the one offense against you in the past 2 years you consider the most serious. (If none in past 2 years, choose the most serious since you were age 55.)
   I have chosen an offense:
   ☐ Occurring in the past 2 years.
   ☐ Occuring more than 2 years ago.
   ☐ I have not been the victim of a crime since I reached age 55.
   (IF NONE, you are finished with this questionnaire. Thank you.)

4. Thinking of the *one most serious* offense, what kind of incident was it?
   ☐ Disturbing the peace
   ☐ Assault
   ☐ Purse Snatch/Pickpocket
   ☐ Theft of property
   ☐ Rape
   ☐ Fraud/Con Game
   ☐ Destruction of property
   ☐ Theft from mailbox
   ☐ Other. Explain: _____

5. Was your home entered against your wishes?
   ☐ Yes ☐ No

6. Were you threatened with harm?
   ☐ Yes ☐ No

Fig. 4.1 (continued)

7. Were you attacked physically?
   ☐ Yes ☐ No
8. Did you lose any money or belongings?
   ☐ Yes ☐ No
9. If you said "Yes" to Question 7 or 8, how much dollar loss did you suffer, including what was taken or demaged, and your medical expenses?
   ☐ Under $50   ☐ $50 to $200
   ☐ $200 to $1000 ☐ Over $1000
10. Did you notify the police?
    ☐ Yes ☐ No
11. If you did not notify the police, why not?
    ☐ I was too frightened.
    ☐ I didn't think they would try to do anything.
    ☐ I thought they wouldn't be able to do anything.
    ☐ I didn't know what number to call.
    ☐ Other. Explain: _____

12. What is the age group of the person or persons who committed the crime?
    ☐ Child ☐ Teenage ☐ Adult
    ☐ Don't know
13. What time of day did it happen?
    ☐ Morning ☐ Afternoon
    ☐ Night
14. How long ago did it happen?
    ☐ In the past twelve months
    ☐ One to two years ago
    ☐ Two to three years ago
    ☐ Three to five years ago
    ☐ Over five years ago
15. Where did it happen?
    ☐ In my apartment
    ☐ In my home
    ☐ In my apartment building
    ☐ In another building or house
    ☐ In a public space in my neighborhood
    ☐ In public elsewhere
    ☐ Other. Explain: _____

This survey instrument was developed for use by police departments to serve as one source of information concerning crime and the senior citizen. The version reproduced here is based upon the experiences of the five demonstration cities. (When reproducing this survey, large type and double spacing should be utilized to facilitate its readability by the senior citizens).

From *The Police Chief* pp. 19, 20 February 1977. Reprinted by permission.

to attend. Also, if the group is a special interest organization, such as retired business people, they may represent a middle-income senior who is not representative of an inner-city senior population. The survey results are not intended for cross-jurisdictional evaluation, but rather for developing individualized crime prevention programs for the group or neighborhood being served.

The survey should help a department to develop stronger links between senior citizens and police officers, and it should also serve as a source of information to assist the police planner, crime prevention officer, and community relations officer in developing and implementing crime prevention programs aimed at reducing the senior citizen's vulnerability and fear.

Implementing the Program
The implementation of crime prevention programs varies depending on participation by, and presentation to the elderly. Seniors must be involved in implementing programs to ensure that the actual presentation will apply to them. For example, because of failing eyesight, many older persons can't read brochures printed in standard type, or older persons may not be able to walk

great distances and, therefore, will require meeting facilities close to public transportation. Another point to be considered is that the actual threat to the older person, as determined through crime reports or other information, may not be the same as the threat perceived by the elderly. Only when the elderly have an input into the planning process can this be determined.

Implementing senior citizen crime prevention programs on a local level should be coordinated, when possible, with local social service agencies serving the elderly. Although the actual crime prevention program may be carried out by police personnel, the input of social service agencies greatly enhances the ability of the police to reach the senior citizen through such programs as "meals on wheels" and neighborhood nutrition sites.

In addition, there is a national network of agencies to serve the elderly comprised of the Administration on Aging and its regional offices, the 56 state and territorial agencies on aging, and over 500 area agencies on aging serving the senior citizen at the local level. In many cases, the area agency on aging is a local or county social service agency. Planning personnel should also try to identify social, civic, religious and retirement groups whose membership is comprised of senior citizens. Housing authority tenant associations may also provide an avenue for reaching low income seniors living in public housing.

Program Evaluation

Program evaluation is necessary to determine if the effort is effective and to indicate needed improvements in implementing it. In some cases, a trial period can be evaluated to refine program techniques. When evaluating such implementation phases, the period of time between pre- and post-measurements should be carefully selected. The measures taken for evaluation should be relevant and reliable. When possible, measures which are objective and quantifiable should be chosen.

The evaluation can basically follow one of two approaches. The first is a highly structured, academic-oriented evaluation methodology which requires personnel who are highly skilled in evaluation design and methods. The second approach is less formal, and often just as useful. It entails estimating the benefits of a program's activities and cost in terms of personnel and other resources. In many cases, the second approach will be preferable. In fact, it was the method used in evaluating the efforts of the five demonstration cities participating in the IACP's model project.

The evaluation questions were designed to identify the nature and scope of the project's activities rather than to measure its specific impact. The evaluation questionnaire is reproduced in Fig. 4.2. The results of this type of evaluation show the orientation of the department as a whole toward the needs of its local senior citizens, as well as the participation of seniors in the department's activities. While this design was intended for use by the IACP in reviewing the work of the five demonstration sites, it could, with minor modifications, serve a

Fig. 4.2 Evaluation Design

(*Note:* Due to space considerations, the questionnaire has been abbreviated to give only the questions asked. In reproducing the questionnaire for use, adequate space/lines should be inserted after each question to accommodate answers.)

This questionnaire has been designed to assist the IACP and the Administration on Aging in their evaluation of this project. Please respond to each of the following questions as completely as possible. These questions are designed to assess the nature of your activities during this project and not to detail the findings or results of those activities. Please attach to this questionnaire copies of any reports prepared as a result of your efforts as part of this project, if you have not already submitted them. You should include your analysis of the Senior Citizen Survey, and any other project documentation which would aid in summarizing your activities.

1. Did you perform a review of those reported crimes whose victim was a senior citizen? If yes, continue with Question 2; if no, proceed to No. 7.
2. What is your definition of a senior citizen?
3. What period of time did this review cover? From _____to _____
4. What crimes were covered in this review?
5. What has been done with the findings of this review? To whom have these findings been distributed?
6. Have these findings been used to reorient the activities of the police department to the needs of the senior citizen? If yes, please explain what actions have been taken; if no, why not?
7. Did you utilize the Senior Citizen Survey prepared by the IACP, with or without modification? If yes, continue with Question 8; if no, proceed to Question 12.
8. How many surveys were completed?
9. During what period of time did you utilize the survey? From _____ to _____
10. How have the findings of the survey been utilized? To whom have these findings been distributed?
11. Have these findings been used to reorient the activities of the police department toward the needs of the senior citizen? If yes, please explain what actions have been taken; if no, why not?
12. Have you implemented special individual oriented crime prevention programs for senior citizens? If yes, please describe.
13. Have you implemented special crime prevention programs for senior citizens involving presentations to groups? If yes, please continue with Question 14; if no, please explain why not and proceed to Question 16.
14. Please list for each program the topic, number of presentations given since this project began, and the average number of attendees.
15. Please describe the type(s) of groups to whom these presentations have been given.
16. Do you utilize senior volunteers in your agency? If yes, please continue with Question 17; if no, please explain why not and then you are finished.
17. Please describe the type of function or service being provided by the seniors.
18. How many seniors participate as volunteers?
19. What is the average number of hours volunteered per day (week or month) per senior?
20. Do these senior volunteers perform a service that would otherwise be performed by a paid individual? If yes, what is that paid individual now doing?
21. Please substantiate, if possible, the cost vs. benefit of your senior volunteer program.

From *The Police Chief*, February 1977. Reprinted by permission.

police administrator, community leader, or criminal justice planning agency in assessing local projects. However, in using such an evaluation design, certain assumptions have to be made. For example, it is assumed that crime prevention programs have a positive effect on enlisting the individual's cooperation with crime prevention activities. If a more definitive measure of the effects or impact of crime prevention presentations is desired, a simple questionnaire can be given prior to and immediately following the program—a pre-test post-test). By comparing the responses, it can be determined what the attendees gained from the presentation. This procedure will enable those presenting the program to determine if they are getting their message across to the participants.

To take this procedure one step further, a similar follow-up questionnaire can be sent to the attendees four to six weeks following the program to determine how much of the information they retained and used. Questions should be added concerning any actions taken or not taken by the seniors and why. For example, "Do you currently use a dead-bolt lock on your doors? yes____ no ____. If not, is it because:

1. it's too expensive,
2. I don't know where to get one,
3. I don't know how to install it,
4. I don't think it will do any good,
5. Other reasons: . . ."

A review of the responses to such questions will provide an insight into the information or assistance needs of the senior, and will identify individuals needing follow-up services.

Types of Prevention Programs

In conjunction with the information previously presented, the following information and examples should assist the law enforcement administrator and crime prevention or community relations officer in determining crime prevention programs most applicable to the needs of local senior citizens. To supplement the information given herein concerning the different types of programs in operation, the *Directory of Crime Prevention Programs for Senior Citizens*—prepared by the author and distributed by the National Criminal Justice Reference Service of the Law Enforcement Assistance Administration, U.S. Department of Justice—provides an overview of 50 senior citizen crime prevention programs in operation during 1975-1977. There are four basic types of crime prevention programs which will be discussed. These include:

1. educational programs,
2. crime prevention assistance programs,
3. victim assistance programs,
4. senior volunteer programs.

Educational Programs. Educational programs are generally designed to present specific information which can be used to reduce both fear of, and vulnerability to, crime. Educational crime prevention programs are the most common type of law enforcement activity directed towards the elderly. In preparing these programs, it is essential to remember that the preventive information to be presented to senior citizens is generally the same as would be presented to a younger audience; a lock is a lock no matter whose door it is on. However, the method of presentation needs to be carefully reviewed. In particular, instructors should take into account the physical capabilities and deficiencies of their audience. For example, instructors must be alert to the speed, volume and enunciation of their presentation so that it is at a level consistent with the attendees' hearing ability. Hand-out materials should also be prepared with the elderly citizen's abilities in mind; type size and style, and paper and ink colors should all be designed so they can be read with ease. Crime prevention audio-visual programs, designed especially for older audiences, have been prepared and should also be used when available.

In addition, older people may be more responsive to the preventative measures described in crime prevention programs if the presentation is made by a fellow senior citizen, either alone or with a police officer. As is true for other areas of specialized law enforcement, police personnel will need training to sensitize them to the particular problems and needs of the elderly. To accomplish this, local resources should be developed to insure availability and low cost. For example, representatives of local social services agencies with backgrounds in gerontology, gerontologists from local colleges and universities, or representatives from the State Office on Aging are possible sources of assistance to the local police executive in sensitizing his personnel to the needs of the aged.

As previously illustrated in Table 4.2, "Crime and the Senior Citizen," a variety of innovative and experimental education programs are currently in operation. In Baltimore, Maryland the police use specially-developed videotapes to identify specific behaviors, skills, and procedures that senior citizens can use to protect themselves against assault, robbery, and burglary. The training design includes discussion and role-playing activities to reinforce the training initiated by the videotaped material. The Police Department of Brigham City, Utah sponsors a monthly luncheon for senior citizens, during which a presentation is made on some aspect of crime prevention, law enforcement techniques, or safety principles. In Evansville, Indiana the Police Department hosts an annual two-day symposium on safety for senior citizens. The California Attorney General's Office offers crime prevention seminars for senior citizens and for professionals working with seniors. In Miami Beach, Florida crime prevention messages are printed on the shopping bags distributed by local groceries. "Pocket the Purse" is a Wilmington, Delaware program designed to convince older women not to carry a purse unless absolutely necessary, and to provide practical alternatives to using a purse.

Crime Prevention Assistance Programs. Crime prevention assistance programs directed toward the elderly include such activities as installing locks, making personal property for ready identification in case of theft, providing escorts at predetermined times for senior citizen group activities, performing home security inspections, and taking part in telephone reassurance projects. Local banks can also perform valuable services to reduce the vulnerability of the elderly through the direct deposit of Social Security checks and the prevention of con games involving the withdrawal of funds. According to the October, 1975 issue of the *Bank Protection Bulletin*, "the Wisconsin Bankers Association says a customer release form may provide added protection for the bank and its customers against various swindle schemes, especially when older customers are the intended victims. WBA says this sample may be reproduced by banks without permission" (Fig. 4.3).

Fig. 4.3 Customer Release Form

The Wisconsin Bankers Association says a customer release form may provide added protection for the bank and its customers against various swindle schemes, especially when older customers are the intended victims. WBA says this sample may be reproduced by banks without permission:

CAUTION

(You are presented with and asked to read and sign this as a courtesy to you. PLEASE READ AND CONSIDER IT CAREFULLY)

The following is to caution you with regard to your request for the lump-sum withdrawal of $ _____ in cash from your account.

This bank does not conduct investigations or verifications of accounts by telephone. (Swindlers often use this method to gain information on accounts, as well as the confidence of their victims.) Nor do police, FBI officials, bank regulatory authorities or bank officials conduct investigations by asking you to withdraw cash from your account for any reason.

Swindlers also often arrange to have you "find" or "help find" a wallet or other valuable. One way or another, they have you put up some amount of money to show your "good faith"—and then depart with the money.

If anyone has presented themselves to you as an FBI agent, bank examiner, police officer, detective or bank official, and requested any information about your account, *or asked you to withdraw any amount from your account,* whether to help them "catch someone" or to show "good faith," or for any other such reason, you are very possibly being swindled.

If any of these circumstances exist, please contact your local police department and have them investigate, *before* you withdraw your money. Remember, swindlers nearly always are friendly and have "honest" faces. They particularly tend to take advantage of older people.

I have read and understand the above statement and the bank has explained it to me. I insist upon the immediate withdrawal in cash.

The form should leave space at the bottom for the signatures of the customer, an officer and a teller.

(This form is reprinted from the October, 1975 issue of the Bank Protection Bulletin with permission of the Insurance and Protective Division of the American Bankers Association. In utilizing this, or any other form, for senior citizens, be sure to use LARGE type to insure its readability.)

From *The Police Chief*, February, 1977, p. 22. Reprinted by permission.

Crime prevention assistance programs in Charleston and Huntington, West Virginia, and in Lithonia, Georgia offer a daily check-in service to senior citizens. If a call is not received from a participant, and if the participating senior can't be reached on the telephone, personnel are dispatched to check on the status of the senior.

Locks and other security devices are provided to eligible senior citizens in South Bend, Indiana; St. Louis, Missouri; and St. Petersburg, Florida. St. Louis employed seniors to do the actual installations.

Victim Assistance Programs. Victim assistance programs deal with the senior citizen after the fact. The intent of these programs is to ease the trauma and the effects of being victimized. Victim assistance activities may involve helping seniors to get follow-up medical assistance, psychological and/or family counseling, emergency funds to replace stolen monies, and replacements of identification and other important papers. Victim assistance programs may be carried out by police and/or social service agencies. In either case, it is vital that the patrol operation and the victim assistance staff maintain close coordination to insure that follow-up services are initiated as soon after the incident as possible.

The New York City Police Department assigns officers to the Office for the Aging's store-front center to counsel and advise the elderly in crime prevention methods. The officers are also there to accept reports of crime and to work with elderly victims immediately after the commission of a crime. In Montgomery County, Maryland the Police Department uses a team approach. A police officer and a social worker provide assistance to elderly victims of crime.

Senior Volunteer Programs. Using senior volunteers in nonhazardous police activities is the program that is least often implemented. However, seniors are currently performing a variety of functions ranging from actually patrolling their own communities to registering bicycles. The roles seniors can play is limited only by the imagination of the crime prevention officer. However, in utilizing senior volunteers, the issue of liability must be addressed. Seniors should be required to bring statements from their doctors attesting to the ability to perform an assigned task, or they should be given a physical exam by the department's physician. Also, appropriate sections of the potential list of liabilities, as listed in Table 4.6 should be reviewed by the department's legal advisor. While this list may seem extensive, a number of the potential liabilities listed are appropriate only to certain tasks which will probably not be engaged in by senior volunteers. In most cases, Section C of Table 4.6 will be the most relevant section to review.

In addition to taking part in nonhazardous police activities, the senior volunteer can function as a liaison between the police department and older citizens in both preventive programs and investigations. Just as female investigators are being used to aid sex offense victims, capable senior volunteers can be used to counsel and comfort older victims of crime.

Senior volunteer programs have been successful in a number of cities. In Cottage Grove, Oregon six trained senior citizens work in the community as

Table 4.6 Possible Liabilities Resulting from the Use of Volunteers (Senior Citizens) in Law Enforcement Functions

This list of possible liabilities was prepared by Michael Korb, supervising attorney with the IACP Legal Development Division, for use by those departments considering the use of senior citizen volunteers.

A. Use of police motor vehicle resulting in personal injury and/or property damage:
   1. To owner, operator, and/or passenger in other vehicles or to pedestrian or owner of other damaged property.
   2. To volunteer driver.
   3. To police officer passenger.
   4. To prisoner passenger.
   5. To volunteer passenger.
   6. To property of police department.

B. Use of personal motor vehicle resulting in personal injury and/or property damage:
   1. To owner, operator, and/or passenger in other vehicles or to pedestrian or owner of other damaged property.
   2. To volunteer driver.
   3. To police officer passenger.
   4. To volunteer passenger.
   5. To property of police department.

C. Personal injury to volunteer while engaged in law enforcement functions (other than the operation of a motor vehicle):
   1. Resulting from own negligence.
   2. Resulting from action of a third party.
   3. Resulting from cause other than own negligence or action of a third party.

D. Personal injury or property damage to a third party resulting from accidental or intentional action of volunteer (other than the operation of a motor vehicle).

E. Violation of the civil rights of a third party.

F. Slander or libel of a third party by volunteer.

G. Violation of terms of contract with union.

H. Performance of duties not authorized or prohibited by law.

I. Liability to spouse for loss of consortium if volunteer killed or severely injured.

Potential Sources of Information to Answer the Above Mentioned Issues

Legal advisor or department counsel.

Insurance agent.

City or county charter or other applicable special act.

General liability insurance policy.

Professional liability insurance policy.

Motor vehicle liability insurance policy.

Workmen's Compensation Act.

Local rules or regulations or court decisions affecting use of volunteers in police activities.

From *The Police Chief*, February, 1977, p. 23. Reprinted by permission.

crime prevention specialists. The 101st Precinct in New York City uses senior citizens to monitor its CB base station in the precinct house. When calls for a police service are received, the seniors forward them to the police dispatcher. Senior volunteers in Mansfield, Ohio work in nonoperational capacities, such as bicycle registration, under the aegis of the police department. In Phoenix, Arizona and Maricopa County Sheriff's Department uses a posse of senior citizens to patrol their own retirement community. The posse members serve as the "eyes and ears" of the department, while regular deputies respond to all required enforcement action.

CONCLUSION

The problem of crime prevention and the senior citizen is an area in which great progress has been made and can continue to be made. The threat of criminal victimization of the elderly has been reduced in a number of communities and, in several cases, this has been a direct result of the active participation of the seniors in the program development and implementation.

The interrelationship of crime, the police, and the older American—long known to the criminal—are now being recognized by the police, social service agencies, and society as a whole. Programs have been developed to reduce the victimization of the elderly, to reduce the impact of crime on the lives of the elderly, and to incorporate the vast resources of the senior population into police service. However, this is an area in which great strides can still be made. This chapter has attempted to provide ideas and tools through which local law enforcement personnel can develop programs to enable their elderly citizens to live in an environment free from fear and to remain active members of their community.

5 Police Investigation With Elderly Citizens

Arnold P. Goldstein
Elizabeth L. Wolf

The elderly citizen who has been burglarized, mugged, flimflammed, involved in an accident, notified about the death of a loved one, or who has experienced some other traumatic event presents special investigative problems to law enforcement personnel. Such a person, whether involved in a dispute, the victim of a crime, the relative or friend of a victim, or even a bystander, may very often become highly emotional, making it difficult for the responding officer to function effectively. The citizen may be confused, disoriented, angry, depressed, hysterical, anxious, fearful, or otherwise highly aroused. In order to conduct an effective investigation, the responding officer first has to calm the highly emotional citizen. Highly emotional people, whether elderly or not, have considerable difficulty providing an officer with the detailed information he needs to conduct a proper investigation, to resolve the complaint, or to apprehend the perpetrator. Once having calmed the emotional elderly citizen, the officer must proceed with his investigation and gather whatever information he deems relevant. In order to accomplish this, he needs to use skilled interviewing techniques. The goal of the present chapter is to aid law enforcement personnel in learning to understand and use this calming-interviewing sequence as effectively as possible. Therefore, step-by-step, detailed descriptions of rapid calming and skilled interviewing techniques are presented.*

---

*Chapter 7 offers an extended description of Structured Learning, a proven method by which law enforcement personnel can be taught these procedures rapidly and lastingly.

The elderly victim of a crime or other event requiring police attention may appropriately be described as a person in crisis, a person who is not thinking clearly, one whose feelings are in control of his reasoning, one whose problem-solving abilities are not working well, and one who is experiencing confusion, arousal, anxiety or anger. How best to calm and interview such persons in crisis has been researched in some detail. Some of this information comes from police officers known to be routinely successful on crisis calls, officers who have specific calming and interviewing procedures when handling such calls. Extended research conducted on other law enforcement personnel has conformed these officers' techniques.* This interview, observational, and research evidence indicates that the effective officer responds to crisis calls involving elderly citizens by using the specific calming and interviewing procedures that follow.

CALMING THE ELDERLY CITIZEN

Give First Impression of a Non-Hostile Authority
The officer's first step in calming the situation is to create an impression of non-hostile authority. How the elderly citizen reacts will, of course, be determined by his or her personality, by his or her history with other police officers, and by the problem itself. However, the officer's behavior, especially his first impression behavior, will have a great deal to do with how the citizen behaves and how cooperative he is with efforts to calm the situation and resolve the problem. As a non-hostile authority figure, the officer takes charge and gives instructions in an understanding yet firm manner; he avoids being too soft or too harsh. The officer who is too gentle in questioning the citizen often fails to achieve his purpose because he has neither gotten the citizen's attention to a sufficient degree nor has he made the citizen feel sufficiently secure or reassured by his presence. On the other hand, the officer who is too harsh may also fail to achieve his purpose because the citizen may become more hostile and upset, thus widening the communication "gap" between them. The officer who is firm, fair, and business-like but not unfriendly is most likely to make a good start toward calming an emotional elderly citizen. He will have established himself as someone who is reliable and in control of the situation.

Show Understanding of the Citizen's Feelings
By his words, tone of voice, facial expression, and gestures, the officer makes it clear to the citizen that he understands accurately what the citizen is feeling and how strongly he is feeling it. For example, "You're really feeling very angry and upset with those teenagers"; or "It can be awfully frightening when something

---

*See Goldstein, A.P., Monti, P.J., Sardino, T.J. & Green, D. *Police Crisis Intervention.* New York: Pergamon Press, 1978.

like this happens"; or "I can understand that you're feeling very sad and alone after a loss like this." If the call involves a dispute between husband and wife, neighbor and neighbor, or landlord and tenant, the officer maintains his impartiality and his professional role by saying: "You're really feeling very angry and upset at them" is an understanding, but neutral statement; "You've got every right to feel angry and upset at them" is a side-taking statement.

Modeling
By these words, tone of voice, facial expression, and gestures, the officer makes it clear to the elderly citizen that he, the officer, is responding calmly to the situation. His calmness and appearance of control can serve as a model for the citizen. By removing his hat, sitting down, and speaking in a normal conversational rate and level while making sure that the citizen can hear him, the officer communicates that he feels no need to be upset, angry, or anxious. This demonstration of calmness frequently has a calming effect on the emotional elderly citizen.

Use Reassurance
In using modeling to calm the situation, the officer's own behavior serves as an example which the citizen can imitate. Using reassurance goes a step further because the officer not only behaves in a calm manner but, in addition, gives the citizen reasons why he, too, should feel calmer. For example, "It will be okay"; "I've handled many calls like this"; "The ambulance will be here very soon"; "The doctor will know how to handle this"; or, "We've got the situation under control." Reassurance is particularly effective if the officer has done a good initial job of establishing a first impression as a non-hostile authority figure.

Encourage Talking
It is very difficult for a citizen to continue yelling, screaming, crying, fighting, or behaving in a highly emotional manner while trying to answer a series of questions being put to him by the officer. Thus, encouraging the citizen to talk is often an effective means of calming him. Sometimes it is useful to encourage the person to ventilate about the problem. The officer asks the citizen to begin at the beginning, and he asks numerous investigative questions regarding exactly who did what, where, in what sequence, and at what time. The officer includes several open-ended questions, and takes notes at a deliberate pace in order to slow down the citizen's rate of talking.

Some citizens, however, will remain upset when encouraged to talk about the problem. They may become more, rather than less, emotional. When this happens, it is often useful to divert the citizen, encouraging him to talk about matters other than the problem. In order to do this, the officer seeks "background information" which he claims he needs for his formal report, such as the names of all the citizens involved, their addresses, ages, phone numbers, occupations, legal relationships, and so forth.

Distraction

At times, an effective means for calming emotional elderly citizens is to divert their attention from the problem in ways other than asking for background information. However, distraction procedures are likely to have a rather temporary effect; thus the officer must be prepared to follow them with other calming procedures if necessary. A citizen may be distracted by asking a favor: "May I get you a glass of water?"; or "May I have a glass of water?" The officer might ask a question that is totally irrelevant to the situation: "Can you tell me where you got that attractive vase?" or "How long have you lived here?" Or he might ask a question irrelevant to the problem situation, but opposite to what the citizen expects: "Would you really prefer to have me stop by later when you've calmed down?" Sometimes an observation totally irrelevant to the problem situation might be offered: "That desk is early 18th century, isn't it?"

Use of Humor

There are citizens with whom the officer can effectively use humor as a calming procedure. At times, humor can put the problem in a more accurate and less serious perspective. It can communicate to the citizen that the officer is not overly upset by the problem (modeling), and it can often cool tempers when the problem is a highly aggressive one.

Repetition and Outshouting

These first seven methods of calming crisis situations may all be considered conversational methods. By using non-hostile authority, showing understanding, modeling, reassuring, encouraging talking, or using distraction or humor, the officer seeks to calm the emotional citizen. One or more of these methods should be used initially by the officer. When these conversational methods fail, a more assertive approach, namely repetition and outshouting should be used.

When individuals are very angry, very anxious, very depressed, or very confused, they are tuned into their own feelings. However, they are often unresponsive to, and even unaware of, the feelings and, sometimes, even the presence of others who are trying to communicate with them. The officer may have to repeat himself several times to "get through" to the citizen. When the citizen's emotion is anger and an altercation is still in progress, the officer may have to outshout the citizen to be heard. This display of authority, or similar steps such as slamming a clip-board loudly often produces an immediate, quieting effect.

Use of Trusted Others

There are crises in which calming the citizen is best handled by means other than the conversational or assertive methods described above. In certain circumstances it may be appropriate for the officer to ask someone else to either assist in, or take full responsibility for, calming the emotional citizen. This someone else often will be a trusted friend, relative, or neighbor of the emotional citizen. Using trusted others as calming sources may prove necessary when the officer is too busy with dangerous or threatening aspects of the police call, when there are too many highly emotional citizens involved for him to handle alone or with his partner, when the citizen is too fearful of police, when the citizen speaks only a foreign language, or when conversational and assertive methods have not succeeded.

Temporarily Ignore

There are times, however, when the effective officer uses none of these procedures, but decides instead to deal with the emotional citizen by temporarily ignoring him. Because of threats to his or a citizen's safety or other emergency aspects of the call, the officer may have to devote priority attention to matters other than the elderly citizen's feelings. An injured person must be given first aid before the hysterical complainant is reassured; or the burglarized premises may have to be secured before the anxious and upset tenant can tell his story to the officer.

While several alternative methods have been presented for calming the anger, anxiety, hysteria or confusion of highly emotional citizens at almost any type of police call, it is not possible to provide specific rules for matching procedures to specific emotions or problems. One police officer may find modeling to be very effective in calming participants in certain situations and in others he may have to resort to outshouting the citizen. A second officer may be excellent at reassuring a senior citizen regarding his problem, while a third may be more effective with other techniques in similar cases. From his own experience, each officer has to decide what works most effectively for him. A competent officer is flexible in his use of these procedures; he realizes that one or two of them cannot work in all situations.

GATHERING RELEVANT INFORMATION

Explaining What the Citizen Should Discuss and Why

Once the situation has been calmed so that the citizens involved can be accurate and reliable sources, the officer begins to gather relevant information. Of course, this information gathering began with his radio call and was supplemented by his observation of people and events as he sought to calm the situation. Now, the officer explains to the citizen what should be discussed and why. The purpose of the interview should be carefully explained to the citizen so that his expectations regarding the needed information are accurate. When he understands what is expected of him, his cooperation is maximized.

Interviewing the Citizen to Get Details
of the Problem as Clearly as Possible

While the main purpose of the officer's interview is to gather relevant information, two other important goals may be accomplished at the same time. If the interview is conducted in a professional manner, the interviewing officer not only obtains maximal amounts of accurate information, but he will also (1) give information about himself and his skills which will maintain the level of emotional calm he built earlier, and (2) build goodwill for himself and the Police Department he represents.

As was true of calming procedures, different interviewing methods are best used for different citizens. Which ones to use at which times will have to be partly decided by each individual officer's own experience in a given situation. We can, however, provide general guidelines. Three sets of interviewing procedures are described below. These are presented here in order of increasing directiveness on the part of the interviewing officer. Thus, open-ended questions and listening, procedures 1 and 2, require much less officer directiveness and assertiveness than confrontation and demanding, procedures 9 and 10.

In general, the officer should begin his interview with the least directive procedures, and make use of increasingly directive procedures as circumstances warrant. While low directiveness procedures suffice in many situations, the very angry, very anxious, or highly confused elderly citizen will require more forceful interview procedures before accurate information can be obtained from him or her. The specific procedures are:

Non-Directive Procedures
   1. Open-ended questions
   2. Listening
   3. Closed-ended questions
   4. Restatement of Content or Paraphrasing
   5. Reflection of Feeling
Moderately Directive Procedures
   6. Selective Inattention and use of Silence
   7. Encouragement and Use of Simplified Invitations
   8. Self-disclosure and Use of Immediacy
Highly Directive Procedures
   9. Confrontation
   10. Demanding

Open-ended Questions. Questions which give the elderly citizen the freedom and opportunity to give an answer of considerable length, an answer shaped mostly by the citizen's wishes and not the officer's, are open-ended questions. These are usually questions which begin with "What," "Why," or "How." "What happened here?" "What do you mean by harassment?" "Why do you describe them as crazy?"

Listening. How well the elderly citizen feels the officer is listening to him or her clearly influences the openness and detail of the citizen's statement. That you are listening is communicated to the citizen both by what you do and what you avoid doing. The skilled listener maintains eye contact, shows by his posture and gestures that he is paying attention, and makes occasional comments to the citizen which also show interest and attention: "I see what you mean," or "I can understand that." Whenever possible, the skilled listener avoids interviewing more than one citizen at a time, reinforces calming procedures as often as necessary, and physically separates witnesses and/or complainants so they can not distract one another.

Closed-ended Questions. Questions which can be answered with "Yes" or "No" or with brief, factual replies are closed-ended questions. These are questions which usually begin with "Do," "Is," or "Are." Such questions are a necessary and valuable part of the officer's interview, and only present a problem when they are used where open-ended questions would be preferable. Closed-ended questions may be inefficient when the officer has to ask a great many of them instead of a few open-ended ones. Closed-ended questions can also be leading questions when they suggest answers.

Restatement of Content or Paraphrasing. This procedure shows the citizen that the officer is paying attention, and it also encourages him to go on and provide further details. The procedure consists of repeating to the citizen, in words somewhat different than his own, the essence of what he has already said: "So you want us to just talk to the youths"; "You're saying you did everything you were supposed to by paying the rent and not making too much noise." Perhaps the most effective use of restatement of content, as far as getting the citizen to provide more details on a given topic, involves restating a single word that is central to that topic. Such words are often presented as a one word question: "Every?" might be used after a citizen stated that something happens every night, and the officer wishes to learn more about the frequency of the problem; "Noisy?" after the same complainant states that he has never had a good night's sleep because of noisy kids, and the officer wishes to learn more about the level of disturbance as perceived by the elderly complainant; "Hopeless?" when the officer is seeking details after a citizen who attempted suicide describes his world as "all black, hopeless and terrible."

Reflection of Feeling. Whereas restatement of content stresses repeating one or more of the facts in the citizen's statement, reflection of feeling focuses on expressing an understanding of the citizen's main feelings. In order to reflect these feelings accurately, the officer must pay attention both to what the citizen is saying and how he is saying it. The citizen who complained that he has never had a good night's sleep because of noisy kids might be told, "You really seem to feel very angry at them and not very hopeful that things will change in the neighborhood." In reflecting the suicidal citizen's feelings, an officer might say, "Everything seems just awful to you, nothing's even slightly hopeful." When people feel that an officer understands their apparent or even somewhat hidden feelings, they are much more likely to continue to provide information.

Selective Inattention and Use of Silence. An excited senior citizen often provides the officer with details of a problem which are irrelevant to what the officer needs in order to take appropriate actions, or, if relevant, in excess of what is needed. In contrast to the citizen who is reluctant, resistive, or silent, the officer may be faced with a victim or a relative who talks too much, and who is difficult to divert to the subject in question. Ignoring irrelevant or excessive statements often is an effective means of stemming the flow. Here the officer should respond in a manner opposite to earlier listening instructions; he should not maintain eye contact, nor should he make understanding gestures and statements which signify he is paying attention.

Encouragement and Use of Simplified Invitations. Elderly people under stress often become quite confused and disorganized in their thinking and speech. Simple officer questions such as "What happened here?" may yield agitated and erroneous answers from such citizens. Under these circumstances it is the officer's task to simplify matters by making his questions very concrete and stepwise. "Encouragement and use of specific and simplified invitations" means the officer must often be a patient questioner, restater, or reflector. He sets up a simplified series of questions and asks them one at a time. He builds his interview with one question or statement logically following the other and he praises the citizen not only for answers but even for trying to answer. In this manner, especially when combined with appropriate calming techniques, the citizen is likely to become less confused and agitated and more accurate and detailed in his statement.

Self-disclosure and Use of Immediacy. People tend to be open with those who are open with them. We tend to share our own thoughts, feelings, ideas, and backgrounds when others reveal such information to us. There are problem situations involving elderly citizens where self-disclosure by the responding officer is a useful interviewing procedure. However, there is an important difference between private self-disclosure and public self-disclosure. Private self-disclosure includes revealing feelings of depression the officer has experienced and any fears he has had in similar situations. Private self-disclosure is not a useful or appropriate interviewing procedure. It tends to diminish the officer in the eyes of the citizen, and it fails to increase citizen self-disclosure. In contrast, public self-disclosure involves the officer revealing information about himself that is relevant to the problem; he might discuss places he has been that are also familiar to the citizen, or types of people he has dealt with.

This moderately directive interview procedure also involves "use of immediacy," a term referring to the disclosure-increasing effects on the citizen as a result of positive officer comments about the immediate relationship formed by the officer and the citizen. The officer who is using immediacy might make comments such as: "I can see just from what you've said so far that you're really trying hard"; or "You make me feel you can be trusted, so maybe you impress other people the same way."

Confrontation. The confronting officer points out any discrepancy in a citizen's statement or any discrepancy between a citizen's statement and his actions. An example of the first, a content-content discrepancy, would be: "You said the youth started it all, but you also said what sounded like he was just minding his own business when you went over to him." The second, a content-feeling discrepancy, is illustrated by: "You told me you want them arrested tonight and you don't care how, but now you're getting upset because you have known them all their lives."

Demanding. If the elderly citizen is very hostile, resistive, or indifferent, the several methods described to this point may all prove unsuccessful. When both non-directive and moderately directive procedures prove inadequate, greater interview directiveness may be required. It is here that the officer's earlier success in creating a first impression of non-hostile authority will pay off. Demanding requires forthright and firm instructions and questioning. The citizen has to tell what he knows, and tell it now! The interviewing officer takes a no-nonsense, business-like—but not hostile—stance, one in which the officer insists rather than asks, tells rather than requests.

Show that You Understand the Citizen's Statements and Give Accurate Answers to His Questions

The citizen being interviewed is most likely to continue providing information if he is shown that the officer understands him. Restatement of content, reflection of feeling, and direct statements to the citizen can be used toward this end. Giving clear, patient, and accurate answers to a citizen's questions also makes an officer's eventual task of taking appropriate action easier. The informed citizen is more likely to cooperate in deciding upon and carrying out the recommended solutions.

In summary, in gathering relevant information, an officer should explain to the citizen what should be discussed and why; he should interview the citizen to get details of the problem as clearly as possible; and he should show understanding of the citizen's statements and give accurate answers to his questions.

In order to be effective with elderly citizens, police investigation must take into account the special needs and characteristics of such citizens. In this chapter a number of calming and interviewing steps and procedures designed for this purpose have been described. By using these procedures, both the responding officer and the elderly citizen find interaction more effective, more pleasant, and more likely to lead to a mutually satisfactory solution of the complaint in question.

6 Assisting the Elderly Victim

Robert Hamel

Three elderly women approached the table. They stopped and began scanning the brochures laid out before them. Suddenly, one of the women looked to the young man and woman, seated behind the table, "How can we feel safe going out at night? How can we feel safe in our own homes anymore?" The young man and woman struggled with the question—the same question that had been asked them at least a dozen times that day, and uncountable times before.

The young man worked with a local Victim-Witness Assistance Program; the young woman with a local Rape Crisis Center. They were staffing an information booth at a local college. The college, in conjunction with community senior citizen's projects and human service agencies, was conducting a Senior Citizens Day in an attempt to inform local elderly persons of services available to them in the community. The questions that were raised by the three elderly women are not unfamiliar to law enforcement and criminal justice personnel throughout the country. The same questions are raised whenever police, or prosecutors, or judges, or members of a victim-witness assistance staff come in contact with groups of elderly citizens.

The significance of the frequence of those questions underscores the pervasive fear of becoming victims of crime held by the elderly. Fear amongst the elderly, and its dominating features, has been well documented by researchers and authors (Clemente & Kleiman, 1976; Goldsmith & Goldsmith,

1976; Goldsmith & Tomas, 1974; Hahn, 1976; Kahana, et al., 1977; Rifai, 1976; Sundeen & Mathieu, 1976). Yet, at the same time, statistical basis for such fear has been lacking (Rifai, 1976). Hahn (1976) and many other authors have repeatedly stated the need for more data on victimization of the elderly.

However, it is the quality of that fear and its psychological impact on the elderly population that is important. Statistics and numbers mirror the quantity of fear but do not reflect the effects of the consuming dread of becoming crime victims. All too often, this consuming fear dictates the way of life for elderly citizens, isolating and inhibiting their activities, and forcing them to make armed fortresses of their homes. Senator Harrison A. Williams has stated the problem most succinctly:

> The sad fact is that millions of older Americans now live under a form of house arrest, barricaded from the outside world. Many are afraid to answer a knock at the door (1975).

THE ELDERLY AND THE POLICE

Fear plays a major role in the relationship between the elderly and law enforcement personnel. Fear, however, is not the only emotion manifested by the elderly. Pre- and post-crime elderly victims demonstrate feelings of loneliness, anger, and powerlessness. These same feelings expressed by both pre- and post-crime victims differ only on a qualitative basis and not on a quantitative one. For example, a 72-year-old widow, with neither children nor close relatives and who has never been victimized, may be in contact with the police three or four times a week. The police act as an umbilical cord to the outside world for this isolated individual. A few moments of support can provide her relief from her loneliness. In cases of past-victimization of the elderly, the degree of emotion appears deeper. Feelings of abandonment add to feelings of loneliness; feelings of absolute vulnerability are coupled with frustration and anger; and all combine to result in an almost all-consuming feeling of powerlessness. Police officers working with elderly victims are often confronted with this mixture of emotions.

Such negative feelings can be, and often are, reinforced by systems that are, supposedly, designed to assist the elderly victim. Frustration and confusion with the criminal justice system often fuel the fires of anger and seem to justify the elderly victim's feelings of helplessness. The lack of adequate supportive services and agencies tends to increase the loneliness and encourage further withdrawal into isolation. In cases of physical injury, elderly victims may be consumed with concern over medical expenses. An increase in awareness of their own vulnerability further adds to the fear of being re-victimized. The result of these emotions can be dramatic, as it was in the case of an octagenarian couple who committed suicide. The couple had spoken little English; they had no relatives; they were totally isolated. The New York City Police found their suicide note, which told of the many times they had been victims of crime, of their feelings of helplessness, of how they no longer felt they could live isolated and terrorized. The couple hung themselves after slashing their wrists.

Police agencies and personnel can and should play a major role in providing a supportive bridge for elderly victims. Law enforcement personnel can help by providing information and alleviating the victim's concerns over involvement with the criminal justice system, by making referrals to supportive agencies, by offering direction and aid in filing for available crime compensation, and by providing immediate intervention and support for the elderly victim.

THE ELDERLY VICTIM AND COMMUNITY SERVICES

The older person may suffer immeasurably as a result of being a crime victim. Clarence Kelley, the former director of the FBI, drew attention to the problem in an article in the *FBI Bulletin*:

> Typically, of course, older persons are among those least able to afford the depredations of crime. Limited financial resources, fixed incomes, and reduced employment opportunities make even a slight monetary loss a catastrophe. Also, physiological factors, attendant to aging, make the elderly more vulnerable and less resilient to the trauma and the personal injury of criminal attack. Accordingly, crime leaves a deeper, more lasting mark, and injuries incurred may be more disabling and require a longer recovery period (1976).

Hahn (1976) attempted to divide the effects of crime against the elderly into four distinctive groups: "(1) Physical damage and suffering; (2) financial cost, and in many cases disaster; (3) emotional trauma, especially fear; and (4) changes in life styles, often involving further withdrawal, isolation and even death."

Senior citizens living on fixed incomes may be confronted with particular hardship in cases in which they have lost money or property as the result of crime. Cunningham (1976) has stated that, "Our research supports strongly the initial assumption that, of all persons who become targets of a criminal act, the elderly usually suffer most ... the elderly victims are usually poor, both relatively and absolutely."

Financial and property loss by elderly victims is especially significant if one considers that those who have least generally lose the most. The urban elderly are by far the most victimized group within the senior citizen population; and they are the ones who, generally, have no savings and are surviving solely on Social Security. A loss of a Social Security check may not only mean the elimination of any rare extras, but may mean the elimination of actual necessities. The following case is offered to illustrate this point.

The New York Telephone Company called the Victim-Witness Assistance Center seeking help for an elderly victim. Repairmen from the company had discovered Mrs. M. when they were dispatched to her home to remove her telephone for nonpayment. The Victim-Witness Assistance Center immediately sent staff members to Mrs. M.'s home.

Mrs. M. is an 82-year-old widow, living alone. Social Security is her only income. In the previous three months she had cashed her check, and on all three occasions been robbed. She had been warned each time not to go to the police. Mrs. M., fearing retaliation, did not report any of the incidents to the police. Instead, she stayed in her home and isolated herself.

When she was contacted, the elderly woman had no food and had not eaten in three days. All utilities had been shut off as a result of non-payment. The Telephone Company had now removed her telephone, also as a result of non-payment.

In this case, as in many others, Mrs. M. was an elderly victim who lived in isolation. As a result of each crime, she withdrew further into her isolation. Fear of retaliation prevented her from contacting the police. She was totally alone. She was unaware of community agencies and services that were available. Further, even if Mrs. M. had been aware of the services, they were unavailable to her because she was disabled. Fortunately, the Victim-Witness Program was able to obtain, through local community agencies, emergency financial assistance and food vouchers. The Program also intervened with the utility and telephone companies to restore heat, lights, and telephone.

Knowledge about the availability of, and the eligibility for, local community services and agencies is extremely important in providing support for elderly crime victims. However, financial problems are not the only hardships confronting senior citizens victimized by crime; the psychological impact may be devastating and, in some cases, permanent. Two further cases illustrate the traumatic effects of crime on the elderly.

Rose, an elderly widow, lived alone in a suburb. In the past, she had opened her door for local youths. Twice they had stolen money and other property. One day two youths broke into Rose's home and demanded money. When she refused, she was severely assaulted.

Rose was hospitalized. Her sister, who lived out of state, had to return to care for her temporarily. However, although Rose healed physically, she began to withdraw and become increasingly depressed. She became more and more dependent on her sister. The withdrawal, a reaction to the assault, became so severe that her sister was forced to sell Rose's house. Rose went to live with her sister, and is now under long-term psychiatric care.

Physical injury as a result of a crime can also result in psychiatric problems.

Mr. L. called Crime Compensation to seek financial assistance. He was referred to the Victim-Witness Assistance Center. Mr. L. had been severely beaten 11 years previously with a lead pipe by five youths. As a result, he was hospitalized with a severe skull fracture. Following several months of treatment, Mr. L. was released and returned to work. Eleven years later he returned to the hospital complaining of recurring headaches and loss of memory. An examination disclosed that he had progressive brain damage as a result of the fracture. Because of the time lapse, Mr. L. was not eligible for Crime Compensation.

Mr. L. will not only incur huge medical expenses, but he will require psychiatric care for the remainder of his life. Community services were made available, and Mr. L. is paying for psychiatric care according to his income.

Rifai (1976) points out the need for community assistance to elderly crime victims. He concludes that, "strong community support networks and family contact can significantly reduce the level of fear and the impact of crime on the older adult." Equally as important is a concerned, informed, and active law enforcement agency that can provide the support and necessary referrals to local agencies.

However, the needs of the elderly are not uncovered only after they have been victims of crime. Law enforcement personnel often encounter older adults in need of financial assistance, support, de-isolation, and housing. The police officers may not encounter these individuals as a result of crime. Any elderly person in need can be helped by an informed and empathic policeman.

The police car responded to the call for assistance from a 68-year-old woman. When they arrived, the two officers found the woman in a wheelchair at the bottom of a long flight of stairs. The elderly woman lived alone and on only rare occasions left her apartment. Usually she found someone to take her up and down the stairs. However, this time she was unable to find anyone capable of bringing her up the stairs. The policemen assisted the woman back to her apartment.

Police intervention would normally end with the filing of a report. However, the attending officers in this case did not allow their intervention to end with their initial contact with this woman. They recognized her extreme vulnerability, and they were aware of services available to isolated senior citizens. Two telephone calls to the appropriate community agencies made by two concerned police officers helped to relocate the woman in a more accessible apartment. She was provided with a telephone, escorts to take her to and from shopping, and assistance in applying for Medicare and other available benefits.

A policeman's sensitivity to the needs of an elderly crime victim can turn a potential tragedy into a positive occurrence.

Officer T. walked into the Victim-Witness Assistance Center office and casually asked if it was the agency that helped crime victims. Officer T. then related his contact with an elderly victim of a robbery. The woman had been robbed of her monthly Social Security money on the way to the grocery store. When he returned her home, Officer T. discovered that the woman was caring for her invalid husband. Upon investigating further, he also discovered that the couple had no food. Apparently, the woman, having cashed her check at the bank, was on her way to the grocery store to purchase the couple's monthly supply of food when the robbery occurred.

The tragedy of this crime was further compounded by the fact that it happened two days before Thanksgiving. However, as a result of Officer T.'s concern, the couple was contacted immediately by community services. They were provided with emergency funding and food vouchers, and were assisted in contacting the appropriate agency to replace the stolen money. They were also given a turkey to brighten up what could have been a bleak and tragic holiday.

Community resources are the keys that unlock doors for many elderly individuals. They are the first step in obtaining assistance. Most police agencies sponsor Senior Citizen Crime Prevention Programs or Senior Citizen Identification Programs. While such efforts are commendable, they are limited in both their effect and their utilization of manpower. It is the "front-line" cop who makes contact with those who most need help. It is the cop on the street who must be sensitive to the needs of the elderly and aware of the availability of community resources.

Community Resources
Some of the most viable services for the elderly are common in most communities.

Victim-Witness Assistance Programs. Such programs are becoming more prevalent across the country. However, they are usually centered in large metropolitan areas because their funding is generally dependent upon the level of crime in the area. They may be located in police departments, prosecutors' offices, probation departments, or social service agencies. They all provide direct services to crime victims. These services generally include information on case status and disposition, transportation to court, information about the criminal justice system, escort and advocacy services, counseling, and, most importantly, assessing the victims' needs and making necessary referrals to community agencies. Any viable Victim Assistance Project will maintain extensive lists of available community services. Further, these programs are multi-faceted and maintain close liaison with all local community service agencies. Victim Assistance Programs should be a valuable resource for law enforcement personnel.

Elderly Victim Assistance Projects. Some states and communities are responding directly to the epidemic increase in crime against the elderly. Governor Hugh Carey, in his State of the State Message to the New York State Legislature, directed funding sources to seek out new programs designed to address the needs of elderly crime victims (1977). The result has been a dramatic increase in assistance and prevention projects for elderly victims. In New York City, the Senior Assistance Project seeks out elderly victims, assists them in filing for

Crime Compensation, and encourages prosecution of offenders. Such programs are particularly important as an aid in securing elderly-specific services from the community.

Crime Compensation Programs. Crime Compensation Programs will be discussed in much greater detail in a later section of this chapter. Some of the more innovative programs have extended their services beyond the simple monetary compensation to crime victims. The New York State Crime Victims Compensation Board has developed a corps of volunteers in New York City to assist elderly crime victims in applying for compensation. The Board has been attempting to expand this concept to communities across New York State. Police agencies are developing similar volunteer projects in collaboration with the Board. This is another way in which law enforcement personnel can become involved in providing services to elderly victims.

Commissions on Aging. Most large cities or populous areas have "umbrella" agencies that administer and fund local senior citizen projects. Such agencies maintain logs of referral sources for the elderly, and can be an invaluable resource in providing appropriate referral services.

Volunteer Action Programs. Probably the most misunderstood, yet most prevalent, of the programs so far discussed are the Volunteer Action programs in the community. The misunderstanding is probably caused by the misnaming of these programs. As a general rule, only part of their function is providing volunteers to local helping agencies; more important, are the massive information and referral systems maintained by these programs. Not only are staff comprehensively trained in resource availability, but also in eligibility requirements for every resource. Further, such programs must have local community ties in order to provide referral assistance. If such a program exists in the community, it is probably the best source of information and referral for local law enforcement personnel.

Senior Citizens Organizations. Almost every community has a senior citizen program. Such programs are sponsored by churches, local governments, and schools. These organizations can be a valuable asset to the officer seeking help for elderly crime victims. Not only can they be an excellent source of information for referrals, but they can also be an important link between the isolated senior citizen and the community. They provide friendship, activities, and security. In searching for assistance, the police officer should not overlook the personal services provided by such programs.

Other Community Resources. In seeking appropriate referral sources, law enforcement personnel should not forget the obvious: churches, senior citizen nutrition sites, local helping agencies, schools, and government agencies. All of these can either provide information or act as community support systems for the elderly crime victim. The ultimate determining factor in providing services will be the level of concern the police officer exhibits—the amount of time he or she is willing to spend in locating services.

Compensation for the Elderly

Senator Mike Mansfield, testifying before the Subcommittee on Criminal Justice (1975), stated, " . . . (that) once society undertakes to furnish protection to its members by way of police and safety facilities, it should, if those protection efforts fail, assume a responsibility for the victim and for his loss."

Senator Mansfield's remarks to Congress were not novel in concept; they were a reiteration of a law written in 1775 B.C. King Hammurabi of ancient Babylonia has often been credited with the establishment of the first compensation program. In the Babylonian Code of Hammurabi, it was written: "If a robber has not been caught, the robbed man shall declare his lost property in the presence of the God, and the city and governor in whose territory and district the robbery was committed, shall replace for him his lost property, and that if it was a life that was lost, the city and governor shall pay one *mina* of silver to his heirs."

The notion of crime victim compensation is neither unique nor new. In fact, the United States has been a relative latecomer in recognizing its fiscal responsibility to citizens who fall prey to violent crime. One ancient African tribal custom dictated that the offender compensate his victim commensurate with the crime: if one tribal member stole another's cow, the thief had to return a cow to the victim; if a hut was burned, the arsonist had to rebuild the victim's hut; if one tribal member stole another's wife, the thief had to replace the victim's lost spouse; and if a man was murdered, the slayer remained in bondage to the murdered man's family for the remainder of his life.

"Civilized" society did not begin to institute comprehensive crime victims' compensation programs until the mid-1960s (Lamborn, 1976). In 1955 Margery Fry, an English penal reformer, called attention to the victims and their need for society's assistance (Viano, 1976). In 1963 New Zealand became the first nation to establish a comprehensive crime compensation tribunal. The tribunal had the authority to make compensatory awards to individuals victimized by certain specified crimes. In 1964 England enacted a nonstatutory crime compensation program. Australia and Sweden have since institutionalized national victim compensation programs; and eight of the ten Canadian provinces have enacted crime compensation legislation.

Since 1975, the federal government of the United States has been attempting to establish a national program for compensating crime victims. To date, while there is federal legislation pending, no national plan for crime compensation exists. Before this chapter goes to press, Congress may have passed the legislation necessary to establish a national Crime Victim's Compensation Board directed by the Attorney General's Office. However, most states throughout the country offer some form of monetary compensation to the victims of violent crime; at present there are over 40 states with either pending legislation to establish crime compensation boards or with already existing compensation programs. State legislators have become increasingly aware of the hardships faced by victims who have sustained serious injuries and incurred extensive medical expenses. As a result, more and more states are proceeding to enact legislation designed to reimburse crime victims for "out-of-pocket" medical expenses. Some states also offer the reimbursement of lost income if the victim is unable to work as a result of injuries sustained during a crime.

The importance of compensation programs to the elderly victim of crime is especially significant because the elderly are particularly susceptible to incurring injuries during the commission of a crime. "Bones are more easily broken and they mend at a much slower pace, if at all. Aches and pains tend to become chronic and longlasting. Existing physical ailments tend to be complicated and increased in severity by the addition of new injuries" (Hahn, 1976). Coupled with the increased likelihood of serious physical injury is the increased difficulty in healing the injuries.

> Mrs. S., a 70-year-old widow, was the victim of a purse snatch attempt by two youths. In the attempt, Mrs. S. was knocked to the pavement, and initially suffered injuries to her right elbow. She was transported to the hospital. While it appeared that Mrs. S. had sustained only minor bruises to her right elbow, upon further examination at the hospital it became apparent that she had also suffered a broken hip. Mrs. S. was required to undergo corrective surgery and months of physical therapy. While the operation was successful, Mrs. S. has since been afflicted with a severe arthritic condition.

For the elderly victim, financial worries over hospital expenses, doctors' bills and prescription costs can be as debilitating as the injury sustained.

> Mr. D., a 73-year-old retired minister was the victim of a brutal burglary. He was held at knifepoint, robbed, and stabbed over 50 times. Mr. D. survived but had to undergo major surgery. He incurred over $40,000 in medical expenses.

Most senior citizens living on fixed incomes cannot afford the cost of private health insurance to cover medical expenses. In the case of Mr. D., his former employers maintained private health insurance for their retired employees; thus most of Mr. D.'s medical expenses were paid by the private medical insurance.

Medicare. The elderly generally have to rely on Medicare for payment of medical expenses. However, Medicare only partially reimburses the victim for his "out-of-pocket" expenditures for medical bills. Medicare covers 80% of medical costs; the remaining 20% has to be paid by the victim. If Mr. D. had not had private health insurance and had been forced to rely totally on Medicare, he would have been financially obliged for medical expenses exceeding $8000. Such a debt could well exceed a full year's income for many of the elderly.

The importance of crime compensation programs becomes even more profound when one considers that many elderly Americans don't have even the minimum coverage that Medicare provides. In working with elderly crime victims, it has become apparent that, despite mass advertising, many isolated senior citizens are not only unaware of their eligibility for Medicare benefits, but are also unaware of the Medicare program itself.

Eligibility. Eligibility requirements for compensation depend entirely on the individual state's laws. Georgia, Nevada, and Alaska have crime compensation statutes that provide relief only to those persons who have been injured while assisting police officers or while trying to prevent a crime; these statutes are referred to as "Good Samaritan Laws." There are also some areas and states that provide compensation to the victim in the form of restitution paid by the offender; such programs exist in Maine, Colorado, and Multnomah County, Oregon. Oregon, however, has five bills pending before the legislature which would appear to ensure the future of a statewide crime compensation program.

Most of the existing programs—outlined in Appendix I—provide full compensation benefits to the "innocent" victims of crime. Further, all the states, with the exception of Florida, have a system for appealing the denial of a filed crime compensation claim.

> Mrs. A., a 78-year-old widow, suffered a broken wrist in an unsuccessful attempt to prevent two burglars from battering down her apartment door. When the burglars did gain entry, Mrs. A. resisted them. They threw her to the floor, causing further injuries to the elderly woman.

While this case appears to have had a legitimate claim for crime compensation, the state's compensation board investigator discovered that Mrs. A. had over $15,000 in a bank account. Her total medical expenses amounted to $160, after 80% of the medical bill had been covered by Medicare. Initially, she was denied compensation because it was ruled that she would not be faced with serious financial hardship as a result of being required to pay the remaining $160. However, the decision has been appealed, and will ultimately be decided by the members of the state's compensation board.

Only those states with restitution projects or Good Samaritan statutes provide compensation for lost, stolen, or damaged property. Most states, except Virginia, with existing programs offer some financial relief to victims who lost earnings as a result of injuries sustained during a crime.

> Mrs. C., 77 years old, had been employed for several years as a domestic worker for a neighborhood family. One day, while going to work, she was knocked to the ground in a purse snatch attempt. As a result, Mrs. C. suffered a broken shoulder and jaw.

The employers had had the foresight to provide private medical insurance for Mrs. C. However, she was forced to miss work as a result of the injuries. She was awarded $229 per month for lost earnings until she was able to return to work. She was also allowed over $400 for medical expenses that were not covered by her own insurance or Medicare.

All states with existing compensation programs offer reimbursement for medical expenses that *are not* covered by private insurance or Medicare; and, in the case of survivors, they will compensate for support and funeral expenses.

> An elderly husband and wife operated a small neighborhood liquor store. In a robbery attempt, the 62-year-old man was shot; he died shortly there-

after. The 61-year-old woman was left alone to manage the store. It closed shortly after the crime.

In this case, prior to the crime, the combined income of the two elderly victims was approximately $500 per month. Following the death of her husband, the widow received financial assistance from various sources, including workmen's compensation. However, the state's crime compensation board awarded her $124 per week in order to bring her income level up to the $500 per month both victims were receiving prior to the death of the husband.

Sam was stabbed to death by his girlfriend. He had no insurance for funeral expenses. His family, a typically poor inner city family, all contributed to the cost of the funeral. His 75-year-old mother, Mrs. C., paid over 50% of the cost.

Mrs. C. was approached by the Victim-Witness Assistance Center and, with its help, filed for crime compensation. In this case, the cost of funeral expenses resulted in a severe financial hardship, not only for the victim's mother but for the entire family. Mrs. C. was awarded the entire cost for the funeral of her son.

While specific details may vary from state to state, generalized eligibility requirements for the existing programs follow a similar pattern.

1. "Generally, any innocent victim of a crime (or good samaritan), who has sustained unreimbursable medical expenses may apply for compensation.

2. Generally, any surviving spouse, dependent, or relative of a victim, killed as the result of a crime, may apply for compensation.

3. Generally, the victim must not have been living with, closely related to, or maintaining a sexual relationship with the offender.

4. Generally, the victim must not have contributed to the situation which resulted in his injury.

5. Generally, residency in the state is not a mandate.

6. Generally, injury involving the use of a motor vehicle, ship, airplane, etc. is precluded except when the vehicle was used as a weapon.

7. Generally, it is not necessary that the offender be convicted, nor is it necessary that he be capable of forming any criminal intent.

8. Generally, most statutes require that the victim suffer undue financial hardship (means test).

9. Generally, the victim is specifically required to offer his or her full cooperation to the law enforcement authorities in the apprehension and conviction of the suspect. And,

10. Generally, the crime must have been reported to the police within 48 or 72 hours" (Skoler, 1976).

As Skoler has described, the outlined eligibility requirements are general considerations in most states offering crime compensation. However, some states have stipulations that either add further restrictions or ameliorate these general eligibility requirements. In Maryland, for example, the Compensation Board reduces awards commensurate with the degree of the victim's questionable conduct and complicity in the crime (Maryland, 1968). In California, Delaware, North Dakota, and Minnesota, either no statute exists relative to the sexual relationship between the victim and offender, or the statute specifically states that such ineligibility can be waived in the furtherance of justice. Living arrangements between the victim and offender are also open to various interpretations. Such was the case of a 72-year-old woman who was raped and stabbed by a boarder in her home. Although the offender was a member of the household, in the strict definition, there existed no degree of consanguinity or affinity between the victim and the offender. The woman was awarded a large sum of money for medical expenses.

Benefits. Benefits and benefit limits are strictly defined under state statutes. Some states offer limited benefits to the victim, while others are mandated to provide compensation for numerous services. New York State compensates the victim for psychiatric care if the severe emotional trauma is the result of a crime.

> Mrs. M., a 67 year old, was brutally raped and sodomized when the offender forced a foreign object into her vagina and rectum. As a result of the crime, the elderly woman suffered a severe mental collapse. She has received, and will continue to receive, the necessary psychiatric care. Mrs. M. has been awarded compensation for the cost of past, present, and future psychiatric therapy.

In Massachusetts, Illinois, Delaware, and Pennsylvania, payments for "pain and suffering" are prohibited. In Tennessee and Nevada, care reimbursement for "suffering and pain" is allowed only in cases of rape.

Most states provide compensation that is negatively correlated with the victim's income. That is, the more income a victim has, the less he will receive in compensation. The principal method used to determine the level of benefits to the victim is the "means test." All state statutes require that monies from collateral and other sources be deducted from awards. The test of an individual's ability to pay his own medical expenses is generally based on his previous year's income tax return and any monies that may be available in bank accounts. The medical coverage that the victim has and benefits that he may be receiving from other agencies or social services are also considered.

> A 60-year-old woman was severely assaulted when two youths broke into her suburban home in a burglary attempt. The woman was hospitalized for four weeks and required follow-up nursing and psychiatric care.

In this case the woman was denied compensation because she was receiving social service allowances, had Medicaid and other insurance which provided her with 100% medical coverage, and lost no income because she was receiving Social Security and pension monies.

In another case, a 61-year-old man was assaulted in a robbery attempt at the motel where he was employed. He suffered several broken bones as a result of the assault. However, crime compensation was denied because the man received workmen's compensation for his injuries and was paid by his employer for the time lost from work.

Barriers. While the benefits provided by crime compensation programs help to alleviate many of the financial hardships for elderly victims, there are many barriers that compensation boards face in their attempts to provide services. As a general rule, state crime compensation boards suffer from a lack of exposure. Many such programs are understaffed, under funded, and under publicized. The result is, of course, that few people in need of the services offered by crime compensation are aware of the existence of such programs.

In New York State, as in many other states, the legislature has appropriated monies for awards and has, at the same time, refused to allot resources to publicize the program. Most compensation boards rely on hospitals, law enforcement, and Victim-Witness Assistance agencies to inform the victim of crime compensation. Law enforcement personnel must take the lead in providing information about compensation to victims. Police officers are usually the first to make contact with the victim; they are the supportive figures in hospital emergency rooms. It takes but a short time to inform an elderly victim of the existence and benefits of crime compensation. However, the time taken can assure victims that they need not worry about burdensome medical expenses.

When they present crime prevention programs to senior citizens groups, law enforcement personnel should include information about crime compensation benefits and should demonstrate how citizems may apply for these benefits. At the same time, they should actively work within these groups to muster support for such programs in states without boards; senior citizens should be encouraged to write in support of appropriate funding and expansion of compensation programs, and to inform others of such programs.

Crime compensation programs should begin to reimburse the elderly for lost property and money. Any loss of money can have a disastrous effect on the elderly who exist on fixed incomes. A stolen television or radio could mean the end of an isolated senior citizen's link with the outside world. Perhaps a formulized "means test" could compensate elderly citizens, at least fractionally, for lost property or money.

Law enforcement personnel should be advocates for the elderly victim. In all states it is incumbent upon the victim to provide the compensation boards with all the necessary information regarding the crime, medical expenditures, amount of lost income, extent of injuries, etc. Such a task can be overwhelming for an elderly victim, especially after he or she has just been the victim of a violent crime. However, a lack of necessary information is reason enough to deny a claim for compensation.

> A 77-year-old widow was knocked to the pavement and brutally assaulted for refusing to give the assailant her purse. She was transported to the hospital, where she was treated for a broken shoulder, a dislocated hip, and a severe concussion. Her medical expenses exceeded $1500.

The woman in this case was denied compensation because she failed to provide the necessary information for crime compensation. The woman was alone, confused, and did not know what information was expected from her.

A 61-year-old liquor store operator opened his door and was shot. He died shortly afterwards. No suspect was ever found, nor was a motive ever uncovered. The survivors were then burdened with funeral expenses.

The claim of the dead victim's survivors was denied because they lacked the information needed by the compensation board.

In every community there are volunteer organizations, hospital social workers, or senior citizens groups that can directly assist elderly victims in collecting the documentation necessary to file for compensation. Law enforcement personnel should provide the link between these agencies and the victims. Many victim assistance projects have a service specifically designed to aid elderly victims in applying for compensation. However, without referral efforts by police agencies, the elderly victims may never come into contact with such advocacy services.

INTERVENING WITH THE ELDERLY CRIME VICTIM

The elderly victim of any crime experiences a great many emotions: fear, anger, depression, frustration, to suggest only a few. The object for expression of these emotions is often the first authority figure the victim encounters, the policeman. These emotional outbursts are being directed at the responding officer because the victim needs to vent his or her feelings. Such displays of emotion are generally not personally directed at the officer, but rather stem from the victim's feelings of helplessness and vulnerability. It is imperative that the policeman remember this point and take immediate action to intervene and provide support.

Anger may beget anger, but it is especially important for the officer to show that he or she is in control of the situation. He must be a solid figure to whom the victim can look for advice and guidance at a crucial moment. While it is essential to gather the facts relating to the crime, it is equally important to reassure the victim. The police officer should begin by dealing with the victim's confusion. The greater the intensity of emotion, the more confusing a situation becomes; and the corollary to this is the more intense the confusion, the more intense the emotions. The problem is self-perpetuating and, unless dealt with immediately, will only compound the police officer's problems.

There are certain rules to be followed when dealing with an emotional elderly citizen. Chapter 5 also gave techniques and procedures.

Rule 1. An officer should be explicit when dealing with the victim. This gives the victim the chance to grab onto some reality: "Sit down in that chair"; or, "Have a drink of this coffee." It also establishes the intervening officer as the figure on whom the victim can rely. Patience and understanding are the principal ingredients in supportive intervention.

Rule 2. An officer should speak to the needs of the elderly victim to restore

the integrity of his security system. The first step might be to offer the telephone number of the police station, thus affording a link to security measures. It
is most important that a police officer remain calm; he should never display
anger to the victim, no matter how angry the crime may make him. An expression of anger can destroy the image of confidence that is needed by the victim.
In long-term intervention with an elderly victim, the goal should be to direct
that person toward returning to, and perhaps improving on, his or her pre-crime
functioning. This can be achieved by bringing helping agencies to the assistance
of the victim.

Rule 3. In follow-up contacts with an elderly victim, an officer should encourage involvement in community programs. Independent action and decision-
making should also be encouraged, but always with support. The police agency
prevention unit should be referred to the victim's home for a security check. If
the elderly victim feels he can maintain the integrity of his home, the need for
dependence can be averted.

Rule 4. An officer should, however, discourage excessive dependence. Extreme dependence on a police officer can be destructive to the victim, and can
become bothersome to the officer. When the police officer is called for every
squeak, patience and empathy can wear extremely thin. Because loneliness and
dependence are almost inseparable, the victim should be encouraged to make
outside contacts with helping agencies and senior citizen organizations. In order
to instill a sense of independence in the elderly victim, some supportive and
follow-up work may be required. The police officer can offer support, assurance,
and a feeling of security by simply making his presence known. This may require
only an occasional telephone call or home visit after the crime to check on
whether agencies have made contact, or whether appropriate security devices
have been installed. The ultimate result will, however, be a greater feeling of
security for the older person.

THE ELDERLY VICTIM AND THE
CRIMINAL JUSTICE SYSTEM

As frustrating and confusing as crime can be to elderly victims, at some point
they may have to enter a system that can create total chaos in their lives. To the
uninitiated, the criminal justice system can be as frustrating and anger-producing
as the crime itself. In order to allay fears, uncertainties, and misconceptions
about the criminal justice system, it would seem to be essential to familiarize the
elderly with the system. The victim is then provided with stable concepts and
may ultimately be a better witness on the stand; in most instances victims are
primary witnesses and an informed witness may be the difference in building a
case. Some of the basics about which a victim should be informed relative to
criminal justice are grounded in common sense: one should never make the

information too technical; and the system should be personalized. If an elderly person asks a question, the officer should never "fake" an answer; instead, he should contact someone who can actually answer the question.

How does one personalize a depersonalized system? The simple act of identifying, by name, those officers involved in the case should provide a bridge between the police investigator and victim. Explaining basic police procedures is an excellent way to clear up confusion and misconception. Above all, the officer should always be honest with the victim; when a burglary victim is erroneously told that chances are excellent for catching the offender, he may react with disappointment and mistrust when the thief is not apprehended. This is especially true of the elderly victim because he is more reliant upon the police.

Preparing a victim for court may be as simple as preparing an informational packet or making an appointment for the victim with the prosecuting attorney. Any informational packet should include a brief outline on police procedures and the court system. The information should be oriented toward familiarizing the victim with a system with which they have never been involved. Fewer surprises will ultimately mean a less anxious witness. The problem has, historically, been that victims or witnesses are pushed through a system they never understood, with even more confusion and negative feelings resulting from their experiences in the criminal justice system.

Developing an informational packet may prove a worthwhile project for any police department's community relations office. Monies may be available for such a project through local service organizations. In any case, the elderly victim should be alerted. He should be advised of the number of court appearances he may have to make, what questions he may be asked in court, and how he can best prepare for court appearances.

Fear is a predominant characteristic of most elderly victims—especially fear of retaliation by the defendant. This fear is further compounded should the victim learn that the defendant was released on bail; even worse, perhaps the victim actually sees the defendant on the street or in the neighborhood. As in most aspects of the criminal justice system, many misconceptions persist regarding bail. In order to prepare the elderly victim for the inevitable, police personnel, in most cases, may be well-advised to take the time to explain bail and the probability of the defendant's release from jail.

In very few cases does retaliation actually occur. Assurance of this fact may well be passed on to the victim by the officer in charge. Further, most states and localities have laws to deal with threats or bribes made by the defendant to a victim or witness; and the severity of such charges may range from a violation to a felony, depending on the particular state statute. This information, coupled with the assurance that police personnel are available, may well serve to alleviate any fear of the victim that may persist.

Information resulting in a little knowledge goes a long way in dispelling myth and misconception. Too often, law enforcement personnel, whether they be prosecutors, judges, or police officers, have had little time to offer victims or witnesses. Unfortunately, such an attitude tends to reinforce myth and misconception, to alienate those people the criminal justice system supposedly protects. It only becomes surprising when a victim refuses to report a crime, or when a witness to a crime refuses to come forward to testify. Patience and understanding are the two essential ingredients in working with any victim, especially an elderly victim.

APPENDIX I

Alaska: Covers medical expenses, burial expenses, and lost earnings. Applicant need not be a state resident. Max. award: $25,000 (medical expenses); $40,000 (lost earnings). Must file within 2 years. Good Samaritan eligibility only.

California: Covers medical expenses, burial expenses, and lost earnings. Applicant must be a state resident. Max. award: $23,000. Includes $3000 limit on job retraining. Must file within 1 year.

Delaware: Covers medical expenses, burial expenses, and lost earnings. Also provides for pension to surviving spouse or dependent. Applicant need not be a state resident. Psychiatric care also included. Min. award: $25; Max. award: $10,000. Must file within 1 year.

Georgia: Covers medical expenses, burial expenses, and lost earnings. Also covers property damage and support of dependents. Applicant need not be a state resident. Max. award: $5,000. Must file within 18 months. Good Samaritan eligibility only.

Hawaii: Covers medical expenses, burial expenses, and lost earnings. Also covers property loss for Good Samaritans. Coverage includes psychiatric care. Max. award: $10,000. Applicant need not be a state resident. Must file within 18 months.

Illinois: Covers medical expenses, burial expenses, and lost earnings. Includes support for dependents. Awards given for treatment by Christian Science Practitioner. Incurred medical expenses must exceed $200. Min. award: $200; Max. award: $10,000. Applicant need not be a state resident. Must file within 2 years.

Kentucky: Covers medical expenses, burial expenses, and lost earnings. Also provides for pension to surviving spouse or dependent. Applicant must be a state resident. Must be minimum of $100 in medical expenses, or two weeks pay, or support. Maximum of $150/week lost income. Min. award: $100; Max. award: $15,000. Must be filed within 90 days but can be extended to 1 year with good cause shown. Crimes committed in prisons and other state institutions are excluded.

Louisiana: (Awaiting passage of federal legislation). Covers medical expenses, burial expenses, and lost earnings. Also includes psychiatric care and support for surviving spouse or dependent. Applicant need not be a state resident. Must incur minimum of $100 in medical expenses or two weeks loss of earnings. Min.: $100; Max.: $50,000. Must be filed within 1 year.

Maryland: Covers medical expenses, burial expenses, and lost earnings. Also includes pension for surviving spouse or dependent. Applicant need not be a state resident. Must incur minimum of $100 in medical expenses or two weeks loss of earnings. Min. award: $100; Max. award: $45,000. Must be filed within 180 days.

Massachusets: Covers medical expenses, burial expenses, and lost earnings. Applicant need not be a state resident. Must incur minimum of $100 in medical expenses or two weeks loss of earnings. Min. award: $100; Max. award: $10,000. Must file within 1 year; 90 days after death of victim. Filing fee: $5.

Michigan: Covers medical expenses, burial expenses, and lost earnings. Also includes pension for surviving spouse or dependent. Applicant need not be a state resident. Max. award: $15,000. Must file within 30 days but can be extended to 1 year for cause.

Minnesota: Covers medical expenses, burial expenses, and lost earnings. Also includes pension for surviving spouse or dependent. Applicant need not be a resident of the state. Must incur minimum of $100 in medical expenses. Min. award: $100; Max. award: $10,000. Must file within one year. Consanguinity restriction waived in the interest of justice.

Nevada: Covers medical expenses, funeral expenses up to $1000, and loss of earnings. Also includes support for surviving spouse or dependent, payment for nonmedical remedial care, and treatment rendered in accordance with a religious method of healing. Applicant need not be a resident of the state. Max. award: $5,000. Must file within 2 years. Special provisions for rape victims. Good Samaritan eligibility only.

New Jersey: Covers medical expenses, funeral expenses, and loss of earnings. Also includes pension for surviving spouse or dependent, and payment for psychiatric care. Applicant need not be resident of the state. Must incur minimum of $100 in medical expenses or two weeks loss of earnings. Min. award: $100. Max. award: $10,000. Must file within 1 year.

New York: Covers medical expenses, funeral expenses, and loss of earnings. Also includes payment for psychiatric care. Applicant need not be state resident. Max. award: $25,000. No limit on medical expenses. Must file within 1 year.

North Dakota: Covers medical expenses, funeral expenses, and loss of earnings. Also includes payment for psychiatric care. Applicant need not be state resident. Support limited to $200 per week. Must incur minimum of $100 in medical expenses. Min. award: $100; Max. award: $25,000. Must file within 1 year.

Ohio: Covers medical expenses, funeral expenses, and loss of earnings. Applicants need not be state residents. Max. award: $50,000. Must file within 1 year. Filing fee: $7.50.

Pennsylvania: Covers medical expenses, funeral expenses, and loss of earnings. Nonresidents compensated only if home state compensates Pennsylvania residents for similar crime. Support limited to $200 per week. Must incur minimum of $100 in medical expenses or 2 weeks in loss of earnings. Min. award: $100. Max. award: $10,000 for injury; $15,000 for death. Must file within 1 year.

Rhode Island: (Awaiting passage of federal legislation). Covers medical expenses, funeral expenses, and loss of earnings; also includes payment for psychiatric care. Applicants need not be state residents. Max. award: $25,000. Must be filed within 2 years.

Tennessee: Covers medical expenses, funeral expenses, and loss of earnings. Includes payment for psychiatric care in cases of sexual crimes. Support is limited to $500 per month. Applicant must be state resident. Must incur minimum of $100 in medical expenses or two weeks loss of earnings. Min. award: $100. Max. award: $10,000. Must be filed within 1 year. Filing fee: $5.

Texas: Covers medical expenses, funeral expenses, and loss of income, not to exceed $150 per week. Also includes pension for surviving spouse or dependent, payment for psychiatric care, and reimbursement for child care not to exceed $30 per child per week up to a maximum of $75/week. Applicant need not be state resident. Max. award: $50,000. Must file within 90 days.

Virginia: Covers medical expenses and funeral expenses only if such will create undue financial hardship. No provision for loss of earnings. Applicant must be a state resident. Must incur a minimum of $100 in medical expenses. Min. award: $100; Max. award: $10,000. Must file within 180 days.

Washington: Covers medical expenses, funeral expenses, and loss of earnings. Also includes pension for surviving spouse or dependent. Provides same benefits under same guidelines as workmen's compensation. Applicants must be state residents. Crimes committed in state institutions or prisons not compensable. Max. award: no limit. Must file within 180 days.

Wisconsin: Covers medical expenses, funeral expenses, and loss of earnings. Provides for pension for surviving spouse or dependent. Also includes payments for psychiatric care and treatment by a Christian Science practitioner. Applicant need not be state resident. Must have incurred minimum of $200 in medical expenses. Min. award: $200; Max. award: $10,000 plus $2,000 for burial and funeral expenses. Must file within 2 years.

REFERENCES

Ann. Code of Maryland Art. 26A, secs. 1-17 (1968).

Clemente, F. & Kleiman, M. Fear of crime among the aged. *The Gerontologist*, 1976, *16*, 207-210.

Cunningham, C. *The Effects of Crime Against the Elderly*. Kansas City, Missouri: Midwest Research Institute, 1974.

Driver, G. & Miles, J. (Eds.) *The Babylonian Laws*. Chicago: University of Chicago Press, 1904.

Goldsmith, J. & Goldsmith, S. Crime and the elderly: An overview. In Goldsmith, J. & Goldsmith, S. (Eds.) *Crime and the Elderly*. Lexington, Mass.: D.C. Heath, 1976.

Goldsmith, J. & Tomas, N.E. Crimes against the elderly: A continuing national crisis. *Aging*, 1974, June-July, 10-13.

Hahn, P. *Crimes Against the Elderly*. Santa Cruz, Calif.: Davis Publishing Co., 1976.

Kahana, E., Laing, J., Felton, B., Fairchild, T. & Harel, Z. Perspectives of aged on victimization, "ageism," and their problems in urban society. *The Gerontologist*, 1977, *17*, 121-129.

Kelley, C. Message from the Director. *FBI Bulletin*, January, 1976.

Lamborn, L. Crime victim compensation: Theory and practice in the second decade. *Victimology*, 1976, *1*, 503-516.

Rifai, M. Older American's crime prevention research project. Multnomah County, Oregon, 1976.

Skoler, G. State victim compensation statutes: A multi-state description and summary. Unpublished paper prepared for the National District Attorneys Association's Commission on Victim-Witness Assistance, 1976.

Sundeen, R. & Mathieu, J. The fear of crime and its consequences among elderly in three urban communities. *The Gerontologist*, 1976, *16*, 211-219.

U.S. Government. Remarks of Senator Mike Mansfield before the Subcommittee on Criminal Justice of the Committee on the Judiciary, U.S. House of Representatives, November 4, 1975. (Serial No. 39, Supplement) U.S. Government Printing Office, Washington, D.C., 1976.

Viano, E. Victimology: The study of the victim. *Victimology*, 1976, *1*, 1-7.

Williams, Senator Harrison A. Statement made at the National Conference on Crime Against the Elderly. *Aging*, 1975, 250,5.

7 Training the Elderly in Mastery of the Environment

Arthur H. Patterson

Much of older Americans' fear about being victimized is related to aspects of their physical and social environment, where they live, and whom they live with.

The purpose of this chapter is to discuss how fear of crime—and actual victimization—among the elderly is related to their physical and social environments, and then to illustrate how the elderly can be helped to gain better control over their environment, thus reducing their fear and their potential for being victimized. Senior citizens can be trained to master their environment; this mastery reduces their fear of crime.

FEAR OF CRIME

Fear of crime among the elderly is growing. A Louis Harris (1975) survey conducted for the National Council on Aging on a national sample of people 65 years of age and older found that fear of crime was rated by 23% of the respondents as their most serious problem. That was even higher than the problem of poor health, which was chosen by 21% of those responding. The poll reported that crime in the streets was the greatest fear among people over 65 years of age. The elderly with poverty level incomes feared crime the most, and elderly women feared crime more than elderly men. Other recent research indicates that the elderly who live alone greatly fear crime, and that the elderly are,

86

in fact, more concerned with their safety than with interacting with other people. An extensive study of Chicagoans 65 years of age or older showed that 41% rated fear of crime as their most serious problem. If one analyzes these and numerous other studies of fear of crime among the elderly, certain patterns begin to emerge. As was suggested in Chapter 2 of this book, there appear to be four major factors which are strongly related to this fear in the elderly: sex, economics, race, and community size.

Elderly women are more afraid than elderly men. This pattern holds true, of course, for the non-elderly as well. However, elderly men and women are more similar in their fear of crime than are non-elderly men and women. This is mainly due to the fact that elderly men are more fearful of being victimized than are non-elderly men.

The lower the economic level of the elderly person, the more fearful of crime that person is. This relationship is readily understandable in light of the fact that the poorer elderly tend to live in declining urban neighborhoods in lower quality conditions, to be in poorer health, and to actually be victimized more than wealthier elderly.

Many studies have shown that black elderly Americans fear crime more than do white elderly Americans. The 1974 Louis Harris survey found that 21% of the white population over 65 years of age, as compared to 41% of the black population, reported crime as a serious personal problem. However, it should be noted that race is highly correlated with economic level; the black elderly tend to be poor. Studies of the more affluent black elderly show that fear of crime more closely resembles that of the more affluent white elderly.

The larger the community, the more fear of crime among the residents. This is true for all age levels, but is particularly true among the elderly. Larger communities result in environments that are conducive to fear, while smaller communities do not. Rural and suburban residents tend to know their neighbors and to have less fear of strangers than do those living in urban areas. Furthermore, urban environments present more potential hazards to the elderly than do rural and suburban environments.

Fear and Victimization

Why has fear of crime been emphasized, as opposed to actual victimization? While only a small segment of the elderly population will ever be the victims of crime, the fear of being victimized touches almost all senior citizens. Further, this fear of being victimized has been shown to have a great and negative impact upon the health, well-being, and behavior of the elderly. Finally, several studies have shown that fear is not necessarily tied to actual victimization. That is, alarm can be high while victimization rates are, in fact, fairly low.

The Impact of Fear

Fear of crime has been shown to lead to profoundly negative effects upon the health, well-being, and behavior of the elderly. Many studies have shown that fear of crime seriously affects where the elderly choose to live. Often senior citizens do not want to move to better housing because they are afraid of the area in which it is located, even though the housing may cost less and provide better amenities and access to services. Similarly, the mobility of the elderly is curtailed by their fear; many are afraid to leave their homes at night, and some are afraid to go out even during the day. It is now recognized that fear keeps many urban old people prisoners in their homes and apartments. This limited mobility affects the social behavior and morale of the elderly, and prevents satisfaction in most other areas of their lives; many do not visit friends, senior centers, or even doctors. These data on fear of crime in the urban elderly closely parallel the research on fear and behavior in crime-ridden public housing projects, where apprehension among the residents also results in decreased mobility, both during the day and at night. This in turn leads to decreased social interaction, lack of community cohesiveness, and feelings of alienation. The ultimate result is poor morale and low life-satisfaction.

In conclusion, it is apparent that a fearful environment leads to a decline in the morale of the elderly. Therefore, feeling safe in and around their homes is one of the keys to their quality of life.

Fear and Control of the Environment

Why are the elderly so fearful of being victimized? Part of the answer involves the loss of control of the environment, both real and imagined, which occurs as people age. Many gerontologists have noted changes in physical skills, psychological traits, and social situations which lead to this loss of control.

B.L. Neugarten (1964) has discussed a personality trait called "active mastery," which describes the extent to which people view themselves as being able to solve their own problems. This is opposed to passivity, where a person accepts problems and tries to adapt to them. Neugarten has shown that middle-aged people are more likely to show active mastery than are older people, and that, in fact, there is a shift in psychological orientation among many older people from active mastery to passivity.

Similarly, M.P. Lawton and his associates (1976) have described how the aging process involves a series of losses. The elderly are often faced with a reduced income, which leads to reduced ability to obtain desired goods and services. Almost 85% of the elderly have some sort of chronic illness, and 12% to 15% are partially or totally disabled. Many suffer from poor nutrition. Many live in poor quality housing, with inadequate transportation and access to needed services. Finally, the older person's social network is continually being reduced through the death of a spouse or a friend and the loss of a job or meaningful social roles.

These conditions lead senior citizens to perceive, in many cases realistically, that they are unable to deal with the threat of a crime. This, naturally, leads to fear. They often doubt their ability to deal with the problem, and feel they have lost control of their environment. This leads them to attempt to adapt to the problem by withdrawing into their residences, which results in reducing their quality of life and diminishing their self-concept.

Fearfulness can be reduced through maintaining some mastery of the environment. In the following sections some of the ways in which senior citizens can maintain this control are examined.

Reducing Fear of Crime

The quality of life of older Americans living in urban areas would be significantly improved if their fear of crime could be reduced. Similarly, reducing their victimization rate would improve their quality of life, both directly through increasing their safety and safeguarding their property, and indirectly through reducing their fear of crime. It is clear that one way to reduce fear and victimization would be through environmental intervention.

Recently there have been attempts to reduce crime through designing environments which reduce the potential for victimization (Rau, 1975). Environments which evoke positive social behaviors from the residents will work to prevent crime. Oscar Newman (1972), an architect and urban planner, carried out a series of studies on this subject for the Law Enforcement Assistance Administration. Newman felt that housing could be arranged so that the residents felt a sense of territorial control and responsibility. Thus, the residents would tend to note the presence and activities of outsiders, and potential criminals would tend to view the dwelling as being under the territorial influence of the residents. While this work on crime prevention through environmental design was not directed at the elderly in particular, it is an approach easily adapted for them. Because the Newman-type approach requires that the resident take an active role in showing control over his or her residence and its environs, it is especially significant for the elderly. As has been discussed, one of the features of aging which leads to fear of crime is a shift in psychological orientation from active mastery to passivity, and a sense of loss of control of one's environment.

TERRITORIALITY AND THE ELDERLY

A recent series of studies has shown that some elderly homeowners do show territorial behavior, and that those who are territorial are less afraid of crime than those who are not territorial (Patterson, 1977). Territorial behavior in this case refers to preserving the physical quality of their housing, building fences or other barriers, using "No Trespassing" or similar signs, and maintaining surveillance of their property. Further, it was found that territorial behaviors were strongly correlated with territorial attitudes. The elderly who had engaged in territorial behavior said that they felt they were in control of their environment. Generally, the more territorial the person was, the less fearful he was.

Environmental Mastery and Fear

The elderly who employ territorial behaviors and who feel in control of their environment are engaging in active mastery of their environment. Since these people are less afraid of being victims of crime than are other elderly, it follows that environmental interventions intended to reduce crime and fear can work for other older Americans. It would appear that the initial step in reducing fear of crime among the elderly would be to find ways to develop active mastery and the feeling of control of the environment.

TRAINING IN ENVIRONMENTAL MASTERY

Training elderly people in environmental mastery can reduce their fears by allowing them to better control their environment; the elderly person can attain and maintain environmental competence. Thus, he can learn to recognize which aspects of the environment are relevant to his goals, and he can use this as the basis for self-initiated actions to promote his personal safety and protect his property. There are many ways the elderly can be helped to be less afraid.

Building Confidence

Because the elderly suffer a decline in positive self-concept as they lose control of their environment, one of the best ways to help them maintain a positive self-concept is to support their confidence in their ability to control through an "environmental support system." Such a system involves all residents, all the business people, and all the service providers of the area. The program is designed to make every effort to support the elderly by making them feel responsible for their own actions, by aiding them in carrying out the actions they choose, and by communicating to them that they are important participants in the life and activities of the area.

Compare such a supportive approach, which helps develop active mastery, with the more traditional community service system. In the traditional system, the elderly are allowed to withdraw from the community; services are delivered to them, whereas they might prefer transportation so that they could seek out goods and services for themselves. Those elderly who live in an area where the environment supports their continued active mastery probably are less fearful than those without such support. An example of this support system is the "neighborhood watch" type of program in which residents are trained and organized to report any unusual or suspicious activities in the neighborhood to the police. This involves the elderly residents, makes them feel useful, and gives them a sense of control over their environment.

Territorial Influence

Because the elderly who are territorial are less afraid of crime than those who are not territorial and because research has shown that territorial control of an area may lead to reduced potential for being victimized, it is important to help senior citizens create areas of territorial influence. There are two approaches to helping the elderly become more territorial: one involves the attitudes of the elderly residents; the other involves their behavior.

Attitudes. In order to develop a feeling of personal responsibility and control over their housing and the surrounding area, elderly residents must feel that their homes are for their exclusive use and control. This feeling of control can result from an effective environmental support system which has gotten the residents actively involved; it can result from getting the elderly person to engage in territorial behavior.

Behavior. When people engage in any behavior, they tend to explain to themselves, or justify, why they did what they did. This leads them to develop an attitude which supports their behavior. Based on that principle, it follows that getting the elderly to engage in territorial behavior will result in their developing feelings of territoriality. If they can be helped to engage in territorial behaviors, they will often begin to feel a sense of ownership and control of their environment. The behaviors can range from simply displaying "No Trespassing" or other such warning signs to actually building fences or other security devices. The key is that the person is actively manipulating his or her environment in order to communicate to outsiders that the residence is under the control, or territorial defense, of the resident. A good technique for getting the elderly to engage in this type of behavior would be to incorporate these suggestions into a program of housing security. This approach could help to provoke territorial behavior, and it could also be an important part of an environmental support system, thus showing the residents that others are helping them to help themselves.

Analyzing the Environment

Another way to reduce fear of crime among the elderly is to aid them in locating and correcting unsafe areas in their environment. Because of the loss of environmental control, many elderly become increasingly affected by their environment. For example, because they are no longer able to drive or can no longer afford a car or taxi, they are dependent upon walking or public transportation for shopping and other services. This can put the elderly in a potentially vulnerable, and definitely fearful, position. They are also placed in this position when they are unable to maintain their homes adequately; cracked windows, broken door locks, and unlighted external areas invite crime. Fear and potential victimization can be reduced by helping them locate and correct these unsafe areas. Clearly some problems, such as an unsafe bus stop, cannot be corrected by the elderly alone. However, by correcting what they can, and by lobbying public officials to correct what they cannot, their feelings of confidence and environmental control can be greatly enhanced. Even if dangerous areas go uncorrected, the very act of locating these areas may help the residents to avoid them and thus feel less fearful.

Perceived Safety

While only a relatively few of the elderly will ever by victims of crime, the fear of being victimized can negatively affect all the elderly. Therefore, educating senior citizens to the realities of crime in their area can lead to more confidence and less fear. Losing active mastery of the environment results, in part, from not being fully informed about that environment. Because of declining physical abilities and withdrawal from social roles, most elderly persons lose some degree of contact with their environment. Personal contacts can give an elderly person the information needed to make behavioral decisions based upon aspects of the environment. For example, the resident who does not know when the bus runs or whether the bus stop is a safe place to wait feels a lack of control and is highly susceptible to fear. In the absence of reliable information, a person may begin to build fantasies based upon stories in the media and rumors in the neighborhood. Often these sources tend to present an inaccurate and frightening perspective on crime (Cook & Cook, 1977).

Educating the elderly to differentiate between real and imagined dangers will help them to feel more competent in their environment. This approach underlies many local crime prevention programs for senior citizens. Initiated by local or state law enforcement agencies, social services and organizations for the aging, and even by private businesses, the programs attempt to reduce victimization and fear by informing the elderly about the aspects of their environment that are related to crime and training them to deal with these elements. These programs include such topics as avoiding street crimes, increasing residential security, being aware of fraud and bunco, developing community cohesion, creating support services such as better transportation, and providing assistance to recent victims of crime. These programs educate the elderly about the reality of crime in their area, and aid them in taking an active role in their own protection. This active role leads to the feeling of active mastery of the environment, which, in turn, reduces fear of victimization.

IMPLICATIONS FOR SERVICE PROVIDERS

Mastery of the environment and fear of crime among the elderly have many implications for those who provide services to the elderly. These service providers include not only members of the criminal justice system, but also public officials, social workers, community organizers, and all the others who attempt to aid the elderly in their daily interaction with the environment. Mastering the environment enhances the well-being of the elderly and facilitates their interactions with the criminal justice system.

Mastery and Well-Being

Recognizing the importance of mastery, or control of the environment, allows providers of services to better meet the needs of the elderly. This is particularly true with regard to crime, where increased environmental mastery has been shown to be associated with reduced fear of crime. Knowing that mastery is related to the well-being of the elderly, and that, with appropriate supports, the elderly are capable of taking environmental responsibility, crime prevention and other programs can be developed that encourage and sustain mastery of the environment. If service providers can help senior citizens to control their own environment, they will see that their work pays dividends.

Facilitating Services

When an elderly person feels competent in coping with his or her environment, that person is also likely to feel better able to cope with the criminal justice system. Some researchers have found that a decreased self-concept can lead older people to view police officers negatively. The older person with a low self-concept may believe that the police do not care about someone as "unimportant" as the elderly (Poister & McDavid, 1976; Sykes & Clark, 1975). He or she either does not seek police aid when it is needed or does not feel reassured when it is offered; thus, such a person tends to remain fearful. If the police officer could help the elderly person to feel more competent, the results would be better interaction and service.

Another aspect of this problem has been discussed by George Sunderland, a former police captain who is now coordinator of crime prevention services for the National Retired Teachers Association—American Association of Retired Persons. Sunderland (1976) has noted that police usually encounter the elderly as victims and witnesses to crimes, or as accident and injury cases. Sunderland believes that there is another possibility for police-elderly interaction; the elderly can be an asset to the police. Active and competent elderly persons can serve as volunteers assisting law enforcement in areas such as home security checks, neighborhood patrols, traffic control, and counseling of victims.

Aiding the elderly to master their environment could help the police in other ways as well. Many of the noncrime uses of police services are the result of a passive rather than environmentally-competent orientation; the police meet those elderly who are either lonely, confused, frightened, or unable to cope by themselves. Reducing the frequency of these encounters could greatly aid police resources. Also, competent elderly make witnesses who are able to provide accurate information and to cope with a complex criminal justice system which involves subpoenas and repeated appearances in court.

Thus, training the elderly to master their environment can greatly facilitate their interaction with the criminal justice system to the benefit of both the citizen and the law enforcement system.

CONCLUSION

Many elderly undergo a shift in psychological orientation from active mastery of the environment to passivity and a loss of control of the environment. This loss of control results in a decreased self-concept and increased vulnerability to victimization and fear of crime. Therefore, it is important to maintain the environmental competence of the elderly as a means of developing safer environments, increasing the well-being of older people, and aiding the criminal justice system.

Providers of services to the elderly can help to develop and maintain environmental competence among these citizens. However, this requires an understanding of the importance of environmental mastery. Further, it requires a working knowledge of service programs that support the older person in acquiring competence and in controlling his or her own environment.

REFERENCES

Cook, F. & Cook, T.D. Evaluating the rhetoric of crisis: A case study of criminal victimization and the elderly. *Social Service Review*, December, 1976, 632-646.

Harris, Louis & Associates. *The myth and reality of aging in America*. National Council on Aging, Washington, D.C., 1975.

Lawton, M.P., Nahemow, L., Yaffee, S. & Feldman, S. Psychological aspects of crime and fear of crime. In J. Goldsmith and S. Goldsmith (Eds.) *Crime and the elderly*. New York: Lexington Books, 1976.

Neugarten, B. and Associates. *Personality in Middle and Late Life*. New York: Atherton, 1964.

Newman, O. *Defensible Space*. New York: Macmillan, 1972.

Patterson, A.H. Fear of crime and territorial behavior in the elderly. Paper presented to Eastern Psychological Association, Boston, April, 1977.

Poister, T. & McDavid, V. A report of Harrisburg resident's evaluations of local government services. Institute for Public Administration, Pennsylvania State University, January, 1976.

Rau, R.M. Crime prevention through environmental design: A historical perspective. Washington, D.C.: National Institute for Law Enforcement and Criminal Justice, 1975.

Sunderland, G. The Older American—Police Problem or Police Asset? *FBI Law Enforcement Bulletin*, 1976, August, 3-8.

Sykes, R. & Clark, J. A theory of deference exchange in police-civilian encounters. *American Journal of Sociology*, 1975, *81*, 584-599.

8 Training Police for Work With the Elderly
Arnold P. Goldstein

This chapter has been written for the police trainer, the person who teaches police officers the appropriate skills for dealing effectively with elderly citizens. What should an officer know, and how can he best learn it? An officer could simply read about calming and interviewing procedures; much of what we all learn comes from "instructional" reading. Thus, trying to learn to calm a confused, agitated, or frightened elderly citizen after reading about how to do so would certainly succeed to some extent. Or, an officer could be asked to listen to a series of lectures dealing with the same content. As is true with reading as a learning method, these lectures could be expected to result in some gains in knowledge.

However, reading and listening to lectures are passive learning techniques. In both instances the officer takes no action, tries out none of the procedures, practices nothing. For this reason, passive learning approaches often fail to bring about either enduring learning or transfer effects. The officer tends to forget what he has learned; or, even if he remembers much of it, he does not know how to apply it where it counts—on an actual call involving an elderly citizen. Thus, a crucial characteristic of the training approach recommended in this chapter is that it requires active learning—learning by doing—by the officer-trainee.

Learning by doing is not the only necessary requirement of effective training approaches, however. "Learning on the road" is also learning by doing, and such learning via the successes and failures of daily patrol experiences is very ineffi-cient and may even be dangerous. Certainly, everyone learns from experience, but it is both a waste of time and effort, and unnecessarily risky, to learn about handling difficult situations by actually trying to handle them. When an officer learns in this way, inefficient, inadequate, or even incompetent police work may result.

Just as the airplane pilot learns by "doing" in a cockpit simulator—in which wasted time is greatly reduced, and real risks to himself and others are essentially eliminated—an effective training approach for police officers also uses simula-tion. It is, to be sure, less "real" than learning at the scene, but, simulated situations in a classroom have been shown to be a rapid and safe way to teach skills which endure and transfer to real-life settings. Thus, the training method we propose requires active learning by trainees, and involves the use of simula-tion in the form of guided and gradual classroom practice and role-playing activities.

The officer who is effective in response to a call involving an elderly citizen is one who has learned a variety of behaviors that produce the desired effects on the individuals involved. The effective officer has not only learned this range of safety, calming, rapport-building, information-gathering, and action-taking behaviors, but he is flexible enough and skilled enough to be able to use the right behaviors with the right citizen at the right time. There are specific procedures that should be followed by those involved in training police officers for effective work with elderly citizens.

STRUCTURED LEARNING TRAINING

Structured Learning Training (SLT) consists of four procedures: modeling, role playing, social reinforcement or other corrective feedback, and transfer training. Each of these has been shown to have a substantial and reliable effect on learn-ing. In each training session, which typically involves two trainers and eight to twelve trainees, the trainees are:

1. played a brief videotape or shown live models depicting the specific skill behaviors that make up effective police action on a call involving an elderly citizen (modeling).

2. given substantial opportunity and encouragement to behaviorally rehearse or practice the effective behaviors shown to them by the models (role playing).

3. provided with corrective feedback in the form of approval or praise as their role playing of the skill behaviors becomes similar to the tape or live model's behavior (social reinforcement). Finally they are

4. asked to participate in all of these procedures in such a way that transfer of the newly-learned behaviors from the training setting to real-life situations will be highly likely (transfer training).

The specifics of how to use this combination of training procedures is presented in step-by-step detail later in this chapter. To aid in most effective understanding and use of these procedures, their background and development, as well as other successful uses to which each has been put, will be described.

Modeling

Modeling, often also called "imitation" or "observational learning," is an effective, reliable, and rapid technique both for learning new behaviors or skills and for strengthening or weakening previously learned behaviors or skills. The variety and sheer number of different behaviors learned, strengthened, or weakened as the result of seeing a model engage in a behavior is quite impressive. Yet, it must be noted that each day most individuals observe dozens and perhaps hundreds of behaviors by others which they do not imitate. In addition to such live models, almost everyone reads a newspaper and watches television every day, and, although he sees very polished models of purchasing behavior, he does not run out to the store to buy the product. In other types of police training, expensively produced, expertly acted, and seemingly persuasive instructional films are shown, but the viewers remain uninstructed. In short, though we are surrounded by all sorts of models engaged in a wide variety of behaviors, we only imitate a very few, and we do so very selectively. Certain factors increase the chances that someone will learn from a model, and these factors are built into SLT. They involve stressing certain model, display, and trainee characteristics.

Model Characteristics. Greater modeling will occur when the person to be imitated, the model, is:
1. friendly and helpful,
2. highly competent,
3. of high rank or status,
4. of the same sex,
5. in control of resources desired by the trainee,
6. rewarded for engaging in the particular behaviors.

Modeling Display Characteristics. Greater modeling will occur when the taped, filmed, or live modeling display shows the models performing:
1. in a vivid and detailed manner,
2. in order from least to most difficult,
3. with considerable repetition,
4. with a minimum of irrelevant details.

Trainee Characteristics. Greater learning by imitation will occur when the trainee:
1. is instructed to imitate,
2. is similar to the model in background or attitudes,
3. likes the model,

4. is rewarded for engaging in the particular behaviors.

If research on the effectiveness of learning by modeling has been so positive, why are the other components of SLT necessary? If so many different behaviors have been altered successfully by having trainees watch and listen to a model, why are role playing, social reinforcement, and transfer training necessary?

The answer is clear. Modeling alone is insufficient because, although it yields many positive learning effects, its effects are often not enduring. The police recruit may watch an experienced officer issue a traffic citation to an angry citizen, and, at that point in time, know how to do so himself. However, if he doesn't take a more active part in the learning process, the trainee is not likely to know how to perform this action effectively for very long. Active participation aids enduring learning.

Structured Learning Training seeks its effectiveness from elements which even go beyond the proven value of active participation. Modeling teaches the trainee *what* to do. To perform what he has observed in an effective and enduring manner, he also needs sufficient practice to know *how* to do it, and sufficient reward to motivate him, or, in effect, tell him *why* he should do it. Modeling shows the *what*; role playing teaches the *how*; and social reinforcement provides the *why*. Each alone is not enough; together, they offer most of what is necessary for effective and enduring learning. The second component of SLT is role playing.

Role Playing

If trainees are to learn how to do something, they must try it. In order to try many behaviors relevant to effective police functioning under safe conditions, there must be a "pretend" quality to the try out. As role playing is used in SLT, this pretend quality is minimized, while a quality of realism is maximized. Officer-trainees do not act out a script prepared for them in advance; following the exact skill steps illustrated in the modeling display, they act out the skill behaviors in the way they think would be most effective and most realistic.

Thus, in SLT, role playing is not just acting, or psychodrama, or general simulation. It is, instead, a behavioral rehearsal that is made real for the trainee in every respect possible. This "rehearsal for reality" quality increases the chances that what the trainee learns in the training setting will be used in the application setting, i.e., in actual situations involving elderly citizens.

A considerable amount of research has been conducted on the effectiveness of role playing as a training technique. In much of this research, a group of people who share certain attitudes are identified, and then divided into three subgroups. One group, the role players, is asked to give speeches which take a position opposite to their real attitudes. The second group, the listen-only group, hears these speeches but makes no speeches of its own. The third group, the control group, neither gives nor hears these speeches. Results of these studies show that role players change their original attitudes toward those proposed in their speeches significantly more than either the listen-only or control groups. Role playing has been shown to contribute effectively to attitude and behavior change in a wide variety of educational, industrial, clinical, and other settings.

As was true in modeling, there are steps that may be taken in conducting role playing to increase the likelihood that it will lead to effective learning. Details concerning the use of these "role-play enhancers" are presented later in this chapter. However, in overview, role playing is more likely to result in trainee learning when the trainee:

1. feels he has some choice about whether or not to participate in the role playing,
2. is committed to his role in the sense that he role plays in front of others who know him,
3. improvises rather than follows a set script,
4. is rewarded or reinforced for his performance.

It was pointed out earlier that modeling is a necessary part of effective training, but that modeling alone is not sufficient for enduring learning. Role playing may also be viewed as a necessary but insufficient training procedure. After seeing effective police action correctly illustrated (modeling), and trying it himself (role playing), the trainee still needs an answer to *why* he should try to learn and use the given negotiation approach. What is his motivation, his incentive, his reward? The trainer's answer to this is social reinforcement.

Social Reinforcement

Psychologists interested in improving the effectiveness of teaching draw an important distinction between acquiring knowledge and actually using it, or between *learning* and *performance*. Learning is knowing what to do and how to do it. Performance is actually doing what we have learned. Modeling teaches what to do; role playing teaches how to do it. Thus, both modeling and role playing affect learning, not performance. Competent performance—in this case, whether the trainee will actually perform what he has learned in the training center—occurs because the trainee receives reward or reinforcement for his role playing.

In SLT both the trainers and the other trainees have the responsibility for giving corrective feedback to the trainee who is role playing. Most of this feedback involves telling the trainee how well he played his role in accordance with the behavioral steps that were modeled earlier. As the trainee's role playing becomes closer to the model's behavior, he receives more positive feedback in the form of approval, praise, and complements. This social reinforcement gives him the motivation and incentive to continue performing well.

Just as there are "rules" which improve the effectiveness of modeling and role playing, there are a number of research findings which can be used to improve the effect of social reinforcement on performance. The effect of reinforcement on performance is increased when:

1. the reinforcement or reward is delivered as soon after the behavior as possible,

2. it is made clear to the trainee which specific behaviors are being reinforced,

3. the nature of the reinforcement being offered is actually perceived as a reward by the trainee,

4. the amount of reinforcement being offered is actually perceived as a reward by the trainee,

5. the trainer reinforces only some performances of the behavior.

At this point in the training sequence, the trainee has learned what to do, practiced how to do it, and has been given the incentive to perform well. What is missing, and what absolutely must be provided, are procedures to increase the chances he will also perform the newly learned skills where they count most—on patrol in the community.

Transfer Training

Transfer training should be a crucial part of any training program. In the training center, away from the pressures of daily patrol and with the helpful support and encouragement of both the trainers and other trainees, most trainees can learn well and perform competently. It is unfortunate that so many training programs accept competent performance in the training center as the criterion for evaluating the success or failure of the program.

While successful trainee performance in the training center is an obvious first step to success outside the center, it is far from a guarantee of it. In fact, more programs fail to transfer than succeed! There are certain transfer training principles that maximize the chances that a trainee will be able to transfer his training gains to the outside world.

General Principles. Transfer of training is increased by providing the trainee with the general principles, reasons, or rules which underlie the procedures and techniques being taught. If the police officer trainee understands *why* certain of his behaviors are likely to lead to certain citizen reactions, he is more likely to know how and when to apply these effective skill behaviors.

Response Availability. The more one has practiced something in the past, the more likely he will be able to perform it correctly when necessary. In many training programs the trainee is required to demonstrate that he can perform a given skill, and once he has done so the trainer moves on to teaching the next skill. Research on "overlearning" clearly shows that this training strategy is an error. Transfer is increased if trainees are required to perform the correct behaviors not once or twice, but many times. Such repetition may seem unnecessary and some trainees even complain of boredom; but the correct skills will be more available if "overlearning" has occurred. Thus, trainees should be encouraged to repeat correct skill behaviors many times.

Identical Elements. The greater the similarity between the training setting and the application setting, the greater the transfer; the more realistic the setting, the better. The ideal training context for police officers should contain many of the same physical and interpersonal characteristics as an actual scene involving an elderly citizen; a simulation setting which is as lifelike as possible should be attempted. The behavior of back-up personnel, perpetrators, victims, bystanders, and others in the training setting should resemble that of their real-life counterparts as much as possible, as should the physical mock-up of the scene.

Performance Feedback. What one does and whether or not he keeps doing it depends a great deal on the evaluations and reactions of other people. A trainee may have learned a skill very well in a training center; he may have been socially reinforced by the trainers there; and he may have been provided with the transfer-enhancers of general principles, overlearning, and identical elements; but the skills may still fail to transfer to the real world. This failure to transfer can and does occur when the real-life evaluators of behavior are either indifferent or critical.

Command personnel, the road-wise and experienced partner, and similar highly credible rewarders can make or break a training program. If such respected sources recognize a trainee's skill behavior with approval, praise, or other social reinforcement, the skill behavior will continue to transfer. If the behavior is either ignored or criticized, it will tend to disappear rapidly. Thus, while a training program can get new skill behaviors started and the other three transfer-enhancers can help keep them going, it is the actual feedback that determines whether or not the behavior continues.

Research in support of this position is so clear that trainers are urged to maximize positive performance feedback by meeting with command and related personnel and training them in what behaviors to look for and encourage, and in what procedures to follow for rewarding skilled and competent behavior. If command support does not exist or if it is indifferent or opposed to the training effort, then the training effort is not worthwhile.

Thus far this chapter has introduced the four procedures which constitute SLT and the means for increasing the effectiveness of these procedures. This combination of training techniques has been used successfully to teach a wide variety of skills to numerous types of trainees: crisis intervention skills to police officers, management skills to those in industry, social skills to shy and reserved persons, disciplining skills to teachers, empathy skills to parents, helper skills to nurses, self-management skills to patients, and negotiation skills to disputants. It is, therefore, appropriate to turn now to the specific and detailed guidelines that a trainer can use when teaching police officers how to deal with elderly citizens.

However, before describing in further detail the procedures involved in organizing and actually running structured learning sessions, it should be mentioned briefly what structured learning is *not*. First, it is important to stress that the skill behaviors portrayed by the taped or live model should not be viewed as the one and only way to enact the skill effectively. The goal is structured learning training is to help build a flexible selection of effective negotiating behaviors which the officer can adjust to the demands of the situation. Thus, while the recommended skill behaviors are good examples, they do not depict the *only* effective way to perform the skills involved.

A second caution for those using the structured learning modeling tapes is that these are not instructional tapes in the usual sense. An instructional tape is most typically played to a passive audience which, at some later date, is supposed to do what was played. Such passive learning is not likely to foster enduring learning.* Thus, the structured learning modeling tapes should not be played without being followed by role playing and feedback. We have demonstrated experimentally that all four components of this training approach are necessary and sufficient for enduring behavior change, and these results should be reflected in the use of these materials and procedures.

Finally, structured learning is not an approach which can be used effectively by all trainers. The knowledge, skills, and sensitivities which a trainer must possess to be effective with this approach are described later in this chapter.

Trainers

The role-playing and feedback activities which make up most of each structured learning session are a series of "action-reaction" sequences in which effective skill behaviors are first rehearsed (role playing), and then critiqued (feedback). Therefore, the trainer must both lead and observe. Because one trainer is very hard pressed to do both of these tasks well at the same time, it is strongly recommended that each session be led by a team of two trainers. Their group leadership skills, interpersonal sensitivity, and enthusiasm are the qualities which appear crucial to the success of training. They must also possess in-depth knowledge of good police procedure, rules, and regulations. If they have had considerable experience with elderly citizens, they will be much more credible to the trainees. In addition to these considerations, structured learning trainers must be especially proficient in two types of skills.

The first might be described as "general trainer skills," those skills required for success in almost any training effort. These include:
1. oral communication and group discussion leadership ability,
2. flexibility and capacity for resourcefulness,
3. physical energy,
4. ability to work under pressure,
5. empathic ability,
6. listening skill,
7. broad knowledge of human behavior.

The second type of requisite skills are "specific trainer skills," those relevant to structured learning in particular. Successful trainers must have in-depth knowledge of structured learning, its background, procedures and goals; they

---

*It is for this same reason, i.e., the inadequacy of passive learning, that we have avoided relying heavily on lectures in our own police training activities.

should be able to orient both trainees and supporting staff to structured learning; they should know how to initiate and sustain role playing; they should have the ability to present material in concrete, behavioral form; they should be able to reduce and "turn around" trainee resistance; they should be well informed on procedures for providing corrective feedback; and they should have group management skills for building cohesiveness and "clique-busting."

For both trainer selection and development purposes, it is most desirable to have potential trainers participate, as if they were actual trainees, in a series of structured learning sessions. They then may co-lead a series of sessions with an experienced trainer, in which they are given several opportunities to practice what they have seen and are provided with feedback regarding their performance. In effect, structured learning can be used to teach structured learning.

The Setting
One major principle for encouraging transfer from the training setting to the real-life setting is the rule of identical elements. This rule states that the more similar the two settings, the greater number of identical physical and social qualities they share, the greater the transfer. Structured learning sessions should be conducted in the same general setting as the real-life environment of most participating trainees; and the training setting should resemble or simulate the likely application setting.

The training room should be arranged to make the structured learning procedures easier. A horseshoe layout, in which chairs are arranged in the shape of a U, is a good example of such a helpful arrangement. The officers playing the roles of responding officer and victim are placed up front and the trainers should place a chalkboard behind and to one side of the role players. Write the specific skill behaviors you're working with at that time on the board so that the officer playing the responding role can see it clearly. The trainees who play the role of responding officer in the staged situation are required to follow and enact the skill's behavioral steps in their role playing. This is a key procedure in structured learning. If possible, other parts of this same room should be furnished—depending on the particular skill being taught—to resemble, at least in rudimentary form, the arrangements of people, furniture, barricades, and equipment which are likely to be found at calls involving elderly citizens. In designing the setting, it is also important to keep in mind the trainees' descriptions of where and with whom they think they would have difficulty performing the skills. When no appropriate furniture or materials are available to set the scene, substitute or even imaginary props can be used.

The First Session
The trainers open the session by introducing themselves; they then have each trainee do likewise. Every trainee should have the opportunity to tell the group something about his or her background and training goals. After the initial

warm-up period, the trainees are provided with a brief description of the program's rationale, training procedures, and skill targets. Typically, a variety of topics are covered: the importance of skills in working with a very wide variety of crimes involving elderly citizens, the value of skill knowledge and flexibility to the trainee himself, and the manner in which training focuses on altering specific behaviors rather than on attitude change are all stressed. Time can be spent discussing these introductory points before the actual training begins.

Modeling

The training begins by playing the first modeling tape or enacting the first live demonstration. To ease trainees into structured learning, tapes or live demonstrations of relatively simple skill behaviors should be used in the first session. Safety skills, consisting of specific skill behaviors which are not difficult for many police officers to enact, would be appropriate here.

All modeling tapes begin with a narrator setting the scene and stating the tape's learning points. Sets of actors—one or two of whom are in the role the trainees are to adopt during later role playing—portray a series of vignettes in which each skill step is clearly enacted in sequence. The narrator then reviews the vignettes, restates the skill steps, and urges their continued use. This sequence—narrator's introduction, modeling scenes, narrator's summary—constitutes the minimum requirement for a satisfactory modeling tape. The format which follows results in more effective modeling tapes and live demonstrations.

I. Narrator's Introduction
   1. Introduction of self
      a. Name and title
      b. Status position, e.g., Chief of Police
   2. Introduction of skill
      a. Name of skill
      b. General (descriptive) definition
      c. Operational (skill steps) definition
   3. Incentive statement—how and why skill-presence may be rewarding
   4. Discrimination statement—examples of skill-absence, and how and why skill-absence may be unrewarding
   5. Repeat statement of skill steps—request attention to what follows.

II. Modeling Displays

A number of vignettes of the skill steps being enacted are presented, each vignette portraying the complete set of steps which make up the given skill. A variety of actors (models) and situations are used. Model characteristics (age, sex, etc.) are similar to typical trainee characteristics. Situation characteristics should also reflect common aspects of calls involving elderly citizens. The displays portray overt model behaviors, as well as ideational and self-instructional—what one says to oneself—skill steps. Models are provided social reward or reinforcement for enacting the skill. The vignettes are presented in order of increasing complexity.

III. Narrator's Summary

1. Repeat statement of skill steps
2. Describe rewards to both models and actual trainees for skill usage
3. Urge observers to enact the skill steps in the structured learning training session and at actual scenes involving elderly citizens

Because of the lack of appropriate equipment, materials, or personnel, the use of modeling videotapes may not be possible. However, an effective structured learning program which teaches effective police skills is still possible; trainers and experienced officers can play the police and citizen roles which make up each skill demonstration.

Each live modeling presentation should be carefully prepared. Scripts must be carefully planned, thoroughly rehearsed, and skillfully enacted before the group. All of the steps which make up a given skill must be clearly portrayed in their proper order. The content of each live modeling demonstration must present a relevant situation in a totally realistic manner, or its effectiveness will be minimal. If adequately planned and portrayed, live modeling can be every bit as effective as videotapes.

The specific skills to be modeled are those procedures described in detail in Chapter 5.

I. Calming the Elderly Citizen

1. Give first impression of non-hostile authority
2. Show understanding of the citizen's feelings
3. Modeling
4. Reassurance
5. Encourage talking
6. Distraction
7. Use of humor
8. Repetition and outshouting
9. Use of trusted others
10. Temporarily ignore

II. Gathering Relevant Information

1. Explain to the citizen what you want him to discuss with you and why
2. Interview the citizen so as to get details of the problem as clearly as possible
   a. Open-ended questions
   b. Listening
   c. Closed-ended questions
   d. Restatement of content (paraphrasing)
   e. Reflection of feeling
   f. Selective inattention and use of silence
   g. Encouragement and use of simplified invitations

     h. Self-disclosure and use of immediacy

     i. Confrontation

     j. Demanding

3. Show that you understand the citizen's statements and give accurate answers to his questions.

Role Playing

A spontaneous discussion usually follows the playing of a modeling tape or the live demonstration of a skill. Trainees comment on the skill steps, the actors, and, very often, on how the situation or skill problem shown might occur in their own work. At this point, the trainees should be divided into groups of two to four, and instructed to prepare for role playing. This preparation is designed to make the role playing as realistic as possible.

The purpose of structured learning is not merely the practice of exercises handed down by someone else; not re-handling old calls but, instead, *behavioral rehearsal*; that is, practice for situations which the trainee is actually likely to face. Each group of four trainees is instructed to develop an event (planning the specific roles of perpetrator(s), victims, relatives, or other citizen) and enact this event as realistically as possible to two other officer-trainees who have been instructed to deal with the call by following the skill illustrated on the modeling tapes or live demonstrations. The specific instructions you give to the trainees preparing the crisis enactment follow.

Role-playing Instructions. Your task during this preparation period will be to design a skit which involves one or more elderly citizens. Afterwards, the skit will be performed with members of your group portraying the perpetrator, victim, and other citizens involved, while one or more members of another group portray a police officer intervening in that situation. All other trainees will then participate in the critique which follows the skit.

The skit requires careful preparation for effectiveness as a learning-teaching method. We suggest you cover the following steps:

1. Talk about cases involving elderly citizens you've known or can imagine; select one that can be effectively portrayed, and that promises to be a good learning vehicle for the audience.

2. Discuss the personalities and situations involved.

3. Select group members to portray the roles.

4. Help the actors become familiar with their roles, with what they will say and do before the "police" arrive.

5. Help the actors practice and become "natural" in their roles. Discourage over..cting. It is *essential* that after the police arrive, your actors react naturally to what the "police" do, and not according to some script. Remember, when your skit is presented, after the intervening officer(s) arrive, the actors should respond to the officer(s) as they think their characters would respond.

As noted earlier, two other trainees are chosen to serve as the responding officers. Their task is to handle the situation effectively by using the several safety, calming, interviewing and action-taking skills which have been demonstrated. All the trainees in the larger group serve as observers. Their later feedback will be used by the two responding officers to further improve their skills.

Before the given role play actually begins, you should deliver the following instructions:

1. *To the two trainees responding to the call (negotiators)*: In responding to the call you are about to hear, follow and enact the relevant skill steps. Do not leave any out, and follow them in the proper sequence.

2. *To the trainees enacting the situation (perpetrator and victim)*: React as naturally as possible to the behavior of the responding officers. Within the one limitation of not endangering anyone's physical safety, it is important that your reactions to the responding officers be as real-life as possible.

3. *To all other trainees (observers)*: Carefully observe how well the responding officers follow the skill steps; and take notes on this for later discussion and feedback.

One of the trainers then instructs the role players to begin. His main responsibility at this point is to be sure that the responding officers keep role playing, and that they try to follow the skill steps while doing so. If they "break role" to comment or explain background events, they should be firmly instructed to resume their roles. As the role play unfolds, one trainer should position himself near the chalkboard and point to each step in turn, being sure none are missed or enacted out of order. If either responder feels the role play is not progressing well and wishes to start it over, this is appropriate. The group should not interrupt until the role play is completed.

The role playing should be continued until all the skits have been presented and all trainees have had an opportunity to participate as responding officers, even if the same skill must carry over to a second or third session. While the skill steps of each role play in the series remain the same, the actual content should change from role play to role play. It is police situations involving elderly citizens as they actually occur, or could occur, which should be the content of the given role play. When completed, each trainee should be better armed to act appropriately in an actual situation.

A few further procedures related to role playing should be pointed out. Role reversal is often a useful role-play procedure. An officer role playing the responding officer may have a difficult time seeing the perpetrator's viewpoint, and vice versa. Having them exchange roles and resume the role playing often helps to change their perspective.

At times, it may be worthwhile for the trainer to take the role of perpetrator in order to show trainees how to handle types of reactions that haven't been role played during the session. It is here that the flexibility and creativity of the trainer is called upon. Finally, role playing at times may become too realistic and the possibility of physical injury to one of the participants may appear likely; in that event it becomes necessary to stop the role playing immediately.

Corrective Feedback/Social Reinforcement

After completing each role play, there should be a brief feedback period. This lets the responders know how well they stayed with the skill steps, or in what ways they departed from them. It also lets them know the psychological impact of their behavior on the perpetrators, and encourages them to try out effective role-play behaviors in real life. To implement this feedback process, certain questions should be asked in the following sequence:

1. *The role-play perpetrator*, i.e., "How did the responding officers make you feel?" "What are you likely to do now?"

2. *The observing trainees*, i.e., "How well were the skill steps followed?" "What *specific* behaviors did you like or dislike?"

3. *The trainers* should comment on how well the steps were followed, and should provide social reinforcement (praise, approval, encouragement) if they were followed closely. In order to provide reinforcement in the most effective manner, trainers should follow certain rules:

a. Reinforcement should be provided *immediately* after role plays which follow the skill steps, and *only* after role plays which follow the skill steps;

b. The specific content of the reinforcements offered should be varied; there should be enough role-playing activity for each group member to have sufficient opportunity to be reinforced;

c. Reinforcement should be given in an amount consistent with the quality of the given role play;

d. When the role play departs significantly from the skill steps, there should be no reinforcement (except for "trying" in the first session or two);

e. In later sessions reinforcement should be spaced out so that not every good role play is reinforced.

4. Finally, *the role-play responders themselves* should comment on their own enactment and on the comments of others.

In all these critiques, it is crucial that the behavioral focus of structured learning be maintained. Comments must point to the presence or absence of specific, concrete behaviors, and not take the form of general evaluative comments or broad generalities. Feedback, of course, may be positive or negative, while a "poor" performance can be praised as "a good try," at the same time, its real faults should be criticized.

If at all possible, trainees who fail to follow the relevant skill steps in their role play should be given the opportunity to re-role play these same steps after they have received corrective feedback. As a further feedback procedure, entire role plays could be audiotaped or videotaped. The "actors" are often too busy "doing" to reflect on their own behavior. Giving them later opportunities to observe themselves on tape can be an effective aid to learning.

Since a prime goal of structured learning is skill flexibility, a role-play trainee who departs markedly from the skill steps may not necessarily be wrong; what he does may, in fact, work in some situations. Trainers should stress that it is an effective "alternative" they are trying to teach, and that the trainee would do well to have it in his repertoire of skill behaviors where it is available when appropriate.

As a final feedback step, after all role playing and discussion of it are completed, the modeling tape should be replayed, or the live demonstration of the particular skill should be repeated. This step, in a sense, summarizes the session and leaves trainees with a final overview of effective skills for dealing with elderly citizens.

Transfer Training

The prime purpose of several aspects of the training sessions described above is to enhance the likelihood that learning in the training setting will transfer to the trainee's actual work environment. Making sure that the trainees in the perpetrator role create an event which is as realistic as possible—both in terms of their own behavior and the physical setting and props of the role play—is one example of an aid to transfer.

Another is to have the two trainees who are in the responder roles for a given skit be two officers who actually work together on the road. Sheer practice increases the chances that what the officers learn in training will be used in the community. Such practice of a skill occurs not only by serving as a responder, but also by serving as either a perpetrator or an observer.

Transfer of training is also a function of the trainee's motivation. "Learning" concerns the question: *Can* he do it? "Performance" is a matter of: *Will* he do it? Trainees will perform as trained if, and only if, they have genuine and active environmental support. Stated simply, new behaviors persist if they are rewarded, and they diminish if they are ignored or actively challenged. Obviously, therefore, a structured learning program should not be undertaken unless some appreciable level of environmental support can be expected from the command and other supervisory personnel.

Reducing Resistance

As happens in all training approaches, some of the trainees who take part in structured learning may be resistive. They may seek to block or avoid the trainer's efforts to conduct the session as it has been defined throughout this chapter. They may argue about the accuracy or relevance of the content of the modeling tape or live demonstration; they may claim that the absence of danger during role playing makes it so different from real life that it is useless; they may show boredom, disinterest, and unconcern. In all, fifteen different ways have been identified in which resistance may occur. These are listed in Table 8.1, along with brief notes mentioning the general approaches for reducing such resistance. Table 8.2 specifically identifies several ways to deal effectively with trainee resistance.

Table 8.1 Types of Trainee Resistance

I. *Active Resistance to Participation*
1. Participation, but not as instructed
2. Refusal to role play
3. Lateness
4. Cutting

Reduce this resistance by: a) encouraging empathically, b) reducing threat, c) instructing.

II. *Inappropriate Behavior*
1. Can't remember
2. Inattention
3. Excessive restlessness

Reduce this resistance by: a) simplifying, b) terminating responses, c) instructing.

III. *Inactivity*
1. Apathy
2. Minimal participation
3. Minimal ability to understand

Reduce this resistance by: a) reducing threat, b) eliciting responses, c) instructing.

IV. *Hyperactivity*
1. Interrupts
2. Monopolizes
3. Trainer's helper
4. Jumping out of role
5. Digresses

Reduce this resistance by: a) encouraging empathically, b) terminating responses, c) reducing threat.

Table 8.2 Methods for Reducing Trainee Resistance

I. *Simplification Methods*
1. Reinforce minimal trainee accomplishment.
2. Shorten the role play.
3. Have the trainee read a script portraying the learning points.
4. Have the trainee play a passive role (or even a non-speaking role) in role playing.

II. *Threat Reduction Methods*
1. Use live modeling of officer role by the trainer.
2. Reassure trainee.
3. Clarify any aspects of the trainee's task which are still unclear.

III. *Elicitation of Responses Method*
1. Call for volunteers.
2. Introduce topics for discussion.
3. Ask specific trainee to participate, preferably choosing someone who has made eye contact with the leader.

IV. *Termination of Responses Methods*
1. Interrupt ongoing behavior.
2. Extinguish through inattention to trainee behavior.
3. Back off contact and get others to participate.
4. Urge trainee to get back on correct track.

Table 8.2 (continued)

V. *Instruction Methods*
  1. Coach and prompt.
  2. Instruct in specific procedures and applications.

VI. *Empathic Encouragement Method (Six Steps)*
  1. Offer the resistant trainee the opportunity to explain in greater detail his reluctance to role play, and listen non-defensively.
  2. Clearly express your understanding of the resistant trainee's feelings.
  3. If appropriate, respond that the trainee's view is a viable alternative.
  4. Present your own view in greater detail, with both supporting reasons and probable outcomes.
  5. Express the appropriateness of delaying a resolution of the trainer-trainee difference.
  6. Urge the trainee to tentatively try to role play the given learning points.

This consideration of trainee resistance and its management completes our presentation of the methods and purposes of the structured learning approach to training police to deal effectively with elderly citizens. Dealing with such citizens requires patient, mature, and skilled police work. We close with the sincere hope that our presentation will contribute in significant ways to the learning of such skills, and thus to rapid and successful police intervention in crime and other situations involving the elderly.

Name Index

Subject Index

PERGAMON GENERAL PSYCHOLOGY SERIES

Editors: Arnold P. Goldstein, *Syracuse University*
Leonard Krasner, *SUNY, Stony Brook*

TITLES IN THE PERGAMON GENERAL PSYCHOLOGY SERIES

The terms of our inspection copy service apply to all the above books. A complete catalogue of all books in the Pergamon International Library is available on request.

The Publisher will be pleased to receive suggestions for revised editions and new titles.